Python for Data Analysis

A Basic Programming Crash Course to Learn Python Data Science Essential Tools, Pandas, and Numpy with Question and Answer from Beginners to Advanced

Oscar Scratch

Table of Contents

Introduction

Congratulations on downloading *Python for Data Analysis* and thank you for doing so.

The following chapters will discuss various aspects of the Python programming language and how it is incorporated in Data Analysis. We will start from the very beginning and give you the historical background of how and when Python began.

We will then go through the various programs that Python uses to complete different functions. A few of the well-known programs include Pandas and Numpy.

Next, we will give you some questions and answers that will be able to answer any questions you may have concerning Python.

And finally, you are shown how to use Python for data analysis along with a few examples of the process.

It is understood that there are plenty of other books that cover this same information all over the internet, but I would like to say thank you again for choosing this one for your learning pleasure.

Enjoy!

Chapter 1: What is Python, Python's History, Basic of Python, Python dictionary, Why Python Data Analysis is so Important? How to Use Python for Data Analysis

Since its organizing in 1991, the Python programming language used to be seen as opening filler, a way to deal with overseeing making a substance that "robotize the getting into stuff". The manner by using which Python handles variable composing. Through default, Python makes use of dynamic or "duck" composing—fantastic for quick coding, yet conceivably thought to boggle in big codebases. That expressed, Python has currently conveyed assistance for non-mandatory unite time kind indicating, so errands that would advantage from static composting can utilize it.

History

Python is a comprehensively utilized well-acknowledged reason, exorbitant level programming language. It modified into at first planned with the aid of Guido van Rossum in 1991 and advanced with the aid of methods for Python programming software premise. It converted into for the most phase superior for accentuation on code intelligibility, and its linguistic structure lets in builders to specific thoughts in fewer tips of code.

How about we burrow further

In the past, due 1980s, records converted into the round to be composed. It changed in that time while taking a shot at Python initiated. Rapidly from that factor forward, Guido Van Rossum started doing its utility genuinely based totally artworks in December of 1989 thru at Centrum Wiskunde and Informatica (CWI) which is organized in Netherland. It transformed into began as a be counted of first significance as an aspect activity venture because of the truth, he was looking for an exciting test to protect him worried sooner or later of Christmas. The programming language which Python is expressed to have succeeded is ABC Programming Language, which had the interfacing with the One-celled critter working framework and had the capacity of exemption overseeing. He had just made ABC ahead of time in his calling and he had unmistakable a couple of problems with ABC anyway supported the majority of the capacities. After that what he did as in reality sharp. He had taken the grammar of ABC, and some of its excellent highlights. It arrived with many objections as well, so he fixed these troubles completely and had made an extraordinary scripting language which had expelled each and every one of the failings.

The motivation for the call originated from the BBC's TV software – 'Monty Python's Flying Carnival', as he grew to become into a huge devotee of the TV application and moreover, he desired a brisk, specific and scarcely secretive require his advent and for this reason, he named it in Python! He used to be the "Kindhearted despot forever" (BDFL) until he ventured down from the association as the boss on twelfth July 2018. For in reality some time he used to work for Google, anyway by using and by, he is working at Dropbox.

The language ends up along these traces propelled in 1991. While it grows to be discharged, it utilized bounty fewer codes to unequivocal the standards, whilst we contrast it and Java, C++ and C. Its sketch reasoning ends up absolutely wonderful as well. Its large objective is to give code lucidity and propelled clothier productiveness. When it used to be discharged it had more than adequate usefulness to provide exercises legacy, more than a few middle measurements type distinctive cases dealing with and highlights.

Python 3.7. Three is the ultra-present day adaptation.

The two of the most utilized renditions wants to Python 2.X and 3.X. There is a ton of contention between the 2 and them to appear to have very some of the unique fan base.

For different purposes comprising of developing, scripting, innovation, and programming, giving it a shot, this language is connected. Because of its magnificence and straightforwardness, pinnacle length places of work like Dropbox, Google, Quora, Mozilla, Hewlett-Packard, Qualcomm, IBM, and Cisco have linked Python.

Python has turned into an extended method to boost to be the well-acknowledged coding language in the global. Python has quite lately developed with growth towards turning into 30, anyway it, in any case, has that obscure intrigue and X part which may be earnestly sizeable from the fact that Google clients have consistently searched for Python a horrendous parcel more than they have scanned for Kim Kardashian, Donald Trump, Tom Journey, and several others.

Python has been a proposition for some other coding dialects, for example, Cobra, Boo, Ruby, ECMAScript, Coffee Script, Awesome, OCami, Julia, quick move
Basic of Python
The Programming language of Python has a broad assortment of linguistic structures, popular library capacities, and intuitive enhancement environment capacities. Cheerfully, you can overlook a massive component of that; you absolutely need to consider ample to keep in contact with some on hand little applications.

You may be that as it may, have to look into some imperative programming requirements sooner than you could do whatever.

Like a wizard-in-preparing, you can also be given these concepts show up to be arcane and monotonous, alternatively with some appreciation and exercise, you may have the alternative to put your PC like an enchantment wand to do stunning accomplishments.

This section has a couple of models that make use of the intuitive shell which is gigantic for examining what essential Python suggestions do, so supply it an endeavor as you see shut by. You'll recall the belongings you enter appreciably higher and more than when you just examine them.

Articulations incorporate characteristics (alongside 2) and administrators (alongside +), and they can normally seem to be at (this is, decrease) right down to an unmarried expense. That implies you may also utilize articulations at any place in Python code that you may additionally likewise make use of an expense.

In the preceding case, 2 + 2 is assessed proper down to a solitary word, 4 A solitary fees without administrators is in like manner concept about an articulation, however, it assesses fantastic to itself, as tested best here:

2

Mistakes are alright!

Applications will crash if they include code the laptop cannot secure, for you to reason Python to reveal a slip-ups message. A goof's message may not break your PC, regardless of the reality that, so do not be reluctant to commit errors. An accident basically implies the application give up taking walks, all of a sudden.

Other performed software program engineers may additionally likewise aspect out that the decent Python code style, Get up and go to start:

"Consistency with the style manual is basic. Be that as it may, in particular: recognize when to be conflicting—every once in a while the style control sincerely does not pursue. If all else fails, utilize your best judgment."

A right element title portrays the facts, it contains. Envision that you moved to some other habitation and named the majority of your transferring pressing holders as Stuff. You'd in no way, shape or form discovers something! The inconsistency of bacon, eggs, and spam can be used like predicting with the fashions of this book as part of a terrible phase made by the documentation of Python (roused with means of capability of the Monty Python "Spam" sketch), anyway in your projects, an expressive title will assist make your code extra discernible.

Python's Dictionary

The Python's dictionary is an unordered accumulation of things. While different compound facts sorts have just fee as a component, a word reference has a key: cost per.

Lexicons are multiplied to get better esteems when the key is known.

How to make a phrase referral?

Making a word reference is as easy as putting things internal wavy supports {} isolated by means of the potential of a comma.

An article has a key and the evaluating really worth communicated as a couple, key: esteem.

While features can be of any facts type and can rehash, keys should be of the changeless sort (string, extend or tuple with unchanging components) and need to be interesting

1.

Void phrase reference

2. my_dict = {}

3.

4. # phrase reference with a wide variety of keys

5. my_dict = {1: 'apple', 2: 'ball'}

6.

7. # word reference with joined keys

8. my_dict = {'name': 'John', 1: [2, 4, 3]}

9.

10. # the utilization of dict()

11. my_dict = dict({1:'apple', 2:'ball'})

12.

13. # from arrangement having each component as a couple

14. my_dict = dict([(1,'apple'), (2,'ball')])

As the need to be apparent above, we can furthermore make a lexicon, making use of the implicit capability dict ().

How to get right of passage to elements from a phrase reference?

While ordering is utilized with different holder varieties to get a section for values, word reference utilizes keys. The key can be utilized both interior rectangular sections or with the get () technique.

The distinction whilst utilizing gate () is that it returns none as a choice of KeyError if the key is by no means once more found.

my_dict = {'name':'Jack', 'age': 26}

Yield: Jack

```
print(my_dict['name'])
```

Yield: 26

```
Print (my_dict. gets ('age'))
```

Attempting to get proper of the section to keys which do not exist tosses blunder

```
# my_dict.get('address')
```

```
# my_dict ['address']
```

When the software is run, the yield will be:

Jack

How to exchange or encompass elements in a Python dictionary?

All of the dictionaries are alterable. We can consist of new contraptions or alternate the measure of modern-day devices utilizing mission administrator.

On the off danger that the key is now present, the price gets refreshed, else any other key: price pair is acquainted with the phrase reference.

How to erase or dispose of elements from a lexicon?

We can discard a unique element in a word reference with the aid of an approach for utilizing the approach pop(). This strategy disposes of an article with the given key and returns the worth.

The strategy, pop item () can be utilized to discard and restore a subjective factor (key, esteem) structure the word reference. Every one of the contraptions can be evacuated on the double the utilization of the unmistakable () technique.

We can furthermore utilize the Del watchword to discard man or woman gadgets or the entire word reference itself.

Python Word reference Strategies

Techniques that are available in phrase reference are arranged beneath. Some of them have just been utilized in the above models.

Technique Portrayal

Clear ()

Evacuate all objects shape the phrase reference.

duplicate()

Return a shallow reproduction of the phrase reference.

from keys(seq[, v])

Return every other lexicon, including its keys from the cost equation and sequence.

Return the estimation of the key. On the off threat that key doesn't leave, return d (defaults to none).

things()

Return any other viewpoint on the word reference's articles (key, esteem).

keys()

Return any other viewpoint on the word reference's keys.

pop(key[,d])

Evacuate the issue with key and return its well worth or d if the key is presently no longer found. In the match that d is presently now not equipped and the key is presently no longer discovered, raises Key Error.

popitem()

Expel and return an arbitrary object (key, esteem). Raises Key Error if the word reference is vacant.

setdefault(key[,d])

In the tournament that key is in the word reference, return its worth. If not, embed key with an estimation of d and return d (defaults to None).

update([other])

Update the word reference with the key/esteem units from another, overwriting existing keys.

values()

Return any other viewpoint on the word reference's traits

Python Word reference Perception

Word reference grasp is an abased, and succinct method to make new lexicon from an iterable in Python.

Word reference appreciation comprises of an articulation pair (key: esteem) considered with the aid of statement inward wavy helps {}.

A word reference recognition can then again include greater for or if explanations.

An optional if revelation can sift through things to structure the new phrase reference.

Other Word reference Activities

Word reference Enrollment Test

We can check if a key is in a lexicon or by no means again utilizing the watchword in. Notice that participation check is for keys, not for qualities.

Emphasizing Through a Word reference

Utilizing a four circle we can emphasize albeit each key in a lexicon.

Worked in Capacities with Lexicon

Worked in capacities like all(), any(), len(), cmp(), arranged() and so on are each now and once more utilized with a lexicon to perform great undertakings.

Function Description

all()

Return Genuine if all keys of the lexicon are proper (or if the phrase reference is vacant).

any()

Return Genuine if any key of the word reference is valid. On the off chance that the phrase reference is vacant, return False.

len()

Return the length (the assortment of things) in the word reference.

cmp() Compares contraptions of two-word references.

arranged()

Return another arranged rundown of keys in the phrase reference.

Why Python Information Investigation is so Significant

The Python language is portrayed by way of a method for its makers as... a deciphered, object-situated, an atypical kingdom programming language with dynamic semantics. Its atypical state worked in record structures, joined with dynamic composing and dynamic official, make it enthralling for Fast

Application Improvement, just as for use as a scripting or paste language to interface modern parts together.

Python is an ordinary cause programming language, that implies it very properly might also be utilized in the enhancement of each and every net and work region application. It's, in addition, helpful in the enhancement of complex numeric and logical applications. With this type of flexibility, it comes as no stun that Python is one of the quickest developing programming dialects on the planet.

So how does Python correspond with document examination? We will take a shut exhibit up about why this flexible programming language is a want to for all people who needs a vacation in realities evaluation today or is looking for some possible roads of upskilling. When you're set, you may have a most excellent instinct regarding, why you need to pick Python for information examination.

Data Analysis or Data Science

Before swimming in too far on why Python is so basic to the analysis of facts, it is vital to initially build up the connection between facts, evaluation and information science, due to the fact that the remaining additionally will in general increase significantly from the programming language. In a range of words, a sizeable range of the intentions Python is gorgeous for documents science furthermore winds up being motives why it's excellent for measurements examination.

The two fields have a great cover, and then again are in addition quite unmistakable, every on their personal right. The integral distinction between data expert and measurements researcher is that the preceding monks' large bits of information from perceived information, while the closing preparations greater noteworthy with the hypotheticals, the what-uncertainties. Information examiners adapt to everyday, the utilization of realities to reply questions added to them, while actualities researchers attempt to count on the future and physique these forecasts in new inquiries. Or then once more to put in some other way, information investigators major focus on the present time and place, whilst insights researchers extrapolate what may additionally be.

There are persistent instances the spot the traces get obscured between the two claims to fame, and that is the purpose the presents that Python gives on measurement science can perhaps be the equal ones delighted in via record examination. For example, the two callings require a knowledge of programming, building, prepared verbal trade aptitudes, predominant math learning, and comprehension of calculations. Besides, each and every calling require mastery of programming dialects, for example, R, SQL, and, obviously, Python.

On the various hand, a certainties researcher needs to in the best world to have a stable project intuition, even though the insights specialist would not like to need to stress overturning into acquainted with that specific ability. In any case, information examiners ought to as an option is being mastered with spreadsheet gear, for example, Exceed expectations.

To the extent pay prices to go, a passage degree information professional can pull in a yearly $60,000 USD income by way of and large, while the documents researcher's middle profit is $122,000 USD in the US and Canada, with facts science directors wages $176,000 USD all matters considered.

So at that point, for what cause IS Python quintessential for information investigation? Well...

• It's Adaptable. On the off risk that you assist to have a go at something imaginative that is now not the slightest bit completed previously, at that point Python is fantastic for you. It's most excellent for developers who choose to content material capacities and sites.

• It's Anything but hard to Learn. On account of Python's focal point of consideration on straightforwardness and intelligibility, it flaunts a steady and shockingly low expectation to absorb information. This simplicity of becoming acquainted with makes Python the best machine for starting developers. Python offers software program engineers the enlarge of the utilization of much fewer pointers of code to reap errands than one desires when the use of extra hooked up dialects. In more than a few words, you invest extra electricity taking part in with it and notably less time managing code.

• It's Open Source. Python is open source, which aptitude, it's free, and uses a network-based mannequin for advancement. Python is supposed to keep going for walks on Windows and Linux situations. Additionally, it can effortlessly be ported to more than one stage. There are many open-source Python libraries, for example, Information control, Information Perception, Insights, Science, AI, and Normal Language Handling, to title essentially a couple (however observe under for more about this).

• It's Well-Upheld. Anything that can go inaccurate will turn out badly, and in case you're the utilization of something that you didn't have to pay for, getting help can be a sizable test. Luckily, Python has a Goliath following and is intensely utilized in scholastic and cutting-edge circles, which potential that there are loads of helpful examination libraries accessible. Python consumers desiring help can commonly flip to Stack Flood, mailing records, and purchaser contributed code and documentation. Furthermore, the greater distinguished famed Python turns into, the more noteworthy consumers will make commitment insights on their consumer experience, and that capability extra help material is reachable at no expense. This makes a self-propagating winding of acknowledgment by methods for a developing assortment of records investigators and information researchers. No surprise Python's notoriety is expanding!

Thus, lengthy story short, Python isn't excessively stressed to utilize, the price is correct (free!) and there is plentiful assist out there to verify that you may not be acquainted with a sudden quit if a problem emerges. That implies, this is one of these super activities were "you get what you pay for" clearly no longer applies!

Step by Step Guidelines to Utilize Python for Data Analysis

Data Science has gotten a notable amount of fame in recent years. This present field's good-sized essential center of attention is to change over necessary insights into advertising and recreation strategies which allows an association to develop.

The realities are spared and appeared into to get in a sensible arrangement. Already solely the top IT businesses had been related to this challenge anyway these days bunches from a various area and fields, for example, web-primarily based business, medical services, fund, and others are the utilization of insights examination.

There are in excess of a couple of equipment handy for facts examination, for example, Hadoop, R programming, SAS, SQL and some more.

Anyway the most renowned and easy to utilize units for measurements investigation is Python. It is recognized as a Swiss Armed pressure blade of the coding scene on account that it supports geared up programming, object-situated programming as accurately as the deliberate programming language and others.

As indicated by means of the StackOverflow review by 2018, Python is the most well-acknowledged programming language on the planet and is furthermore recognized as the most suitable language for records science hardware and applications.

Python moreover gained the coronary coronary heart of producers in the Hackerrank 2018 engineer overview which is seemed in their affection abhor record.

Python: The Best Fit for Data Science

Python has a one of a type ascribe and is convenient to make use of with regards to quantitative and expository figuring. It is an industry boss for sincerely some time now and is as a rule considerably utilized in extra of a couple of fields like oil and gas, signal preparing, account, and others.

Further, Python has been utilized to supply a lift to Google's inside basis and in creating applications like YouTube.

Data Science Python is comprehensively utilized and is a favored system along being an adaptable and publicly released language. Its significant libraries are utilized for data control and are convenient to seem to be at notwithstanding for a newbie statistics investigator.

Aside from being a fair-minded stage it moreover without the bother contains with any existing framework which can be utilized to take care of the most convoluted issues.

A giant portion of the banks use it for crunching data, foundations utilized it for appreciation and handling, and local weather figure associations like Forecastwatch examination likewise use it.

For what motive is Python desired over other records science apparatuses?

Groundbreaking and Simple to make use of – Python is viewed as a learner language and any researcher or analyst with truly simple records can begin chipping away at it.

Time spent on troubleshooting codes and on exceptional programming, designing limitations is furthermore limited.

As rather than other programming dialects, for example, C, Java, and C# the best opportunity for code execution are less which enables designers and programming to program professionals to invest extra energy to work on their calculations.

Selection of Libraries – Python bears an enormous database of libraries and a counterfeit cerebrum and work area learning.

Probably the most familiar libraries comprise of Scikit Learn, TensorFlow, Seaborn, Pytorch, Matplotlib and some more.

Numerous actualities science and PC examining educational workout routines and assets are close by way of on-line which can be without issues gotten to.

Adaptability – as hostile to different programming dialects like Java and R, Python has substantiated itself as a, particularly versatile and faster language.

It presents adaptability to remedy issues which cannot be explained the utilization of other programming dialects. Numerous gatherings use it to improve rapid functions and equipment of varied types.

Perception and Illustrations – There are extraordinary representation decisions handy on Python. Its library Matplotlib affords a solid premise spherical which a number of libraries like ggplot, pandas plotting, pytorch, and others are assembled.

These applications help to make outlines, web-prepared plots, graphical formats, and so on.

How Python is utilized in each phase of Data Science and Examination?

The Primary Stage – Right off the bat we need to fathom and recognize what sort of shape is completed a certainties take. In the tournament we think about consideration realities as a big exceed expectations sheet with thousand of lines and sections, at that factor you need to comprehend how to control it?

You need to infer experiences through the capability of playing out certain highlights and searching for a precise type of facts in every line as it should be as a section.

It can devour a ton of time and severe work to whole this kind of computational errand. Consequently, you can make use of the libraries of Python like Pandas and Numpy which can in a matter of seconds play out the exercise via the method for the utilization of parallel handling.

The Subsequent Stage – The following obstacle is getting the quintessential data. As facts are presently not continuously

easily close via to us, we want to scratch records from the net appropriately. Here the libraries of Python Scrapy and BeautifulSoup can extricate actualities from the web.

The Third Stage – At this stage, we need to get the understanding of the graphical portrayal of the information. It winds up tough to weight experiences when you see such massive numbers of numbers on the screen.

The terrific approach to do this with the good of talking to insights into the kinds of diagrams, pie outlines, and a number of organizations. To play out this trademark the libraries of Python Seaborn and Matplotlib are utilized.

The Fourth Stage – The subsequent stage is work vicinity becoming acquainted with, which is an especially complex computational procedure. It incorporates arithmetic apparatuses like likelihood, math and grid elements of over thousand sections and lines.

The majority of this can end up being notable simple and circumstance amicable the utilization of the laptop inspecting library Scikit-Learn about Python.

The majority of the referenced advances have been about facts as printed content anyway imagine a scenario the place it is in the structure of pictures. Python is all-around equipped to deal with this sort of things to do too. It has an openly provide library OpenCV which is submitted notably for photo preparing.

Python's Fame in Information Science Gatherings and Networks

Python's similarity and tremendous to utilize sentence structure make it the most prevalent language in the realities of science networks and gatherings. The men and women who have not constructed and science chronicled past can likewise seem at with inside a brisk time.

It is most excellent for prototyping and AI and the accessibility of online publications which is reasonable for fledglings. Its adaptability and beneficial to become aware of making Python the most regarded for after-abilities that full-size companies are searching in an insights science proficient.

The profound acing systems in its APIs close by with its logical applications makes Python excellent gainful.

As per the website online Towards Information Science, in a definitive two years, there has been an excellent deal of progress and advancement in light of the truth that the dispatch of the library TensorFlow. It is additionally expressed that the spot synthetic brain takes an exceptional deal of research, one can approve their ideas in only twenty code lines in Python.

Researchers working with AI and engineers additionally settle on Python for structure functions and tools like assumption examination and NLP (normal language handling).

Chapter 2: How to Improve Your Skills Using Python Programming Language? Why You Can Use it for Improve Your Business? What's a Python Trick? Essential Tools with Python Data Analysis

Python helps the use of modules and packages, which suggest that programs can be designed in a modular style and code, can be reused across a variety of projects. Once you've developed a module or package you need, it can be scaled for use in different projects, and it's handy to import or export these modules.

Follow these wonderful tips; it will assist you to enhance your python programming skills.

Analyze the trouble clearly

Firstly, you need to analyze your trouble very clearly. You need to rethink twice about how to resolve that problem. Sure, you find the answer to that problem.

Collect entire requirements

You need to take the time to write down what desires the product will want to achieve. It will retailer your time to locate the solution.

Create a format or diagram

• For a small project, you want to create a simple flow chart or an easy plan.

• As with for large projects, it helps to break-up the job into modules and to think about the following:

• What undertaking every module ought to perform

• How data gets received between modules

• How the facts will be used within each module

• Although gathering and planning requirements can be more tedious and much less fun than diving straight into coding, it is even greater tedious to spend hours debugging. Take the time to sketch the drift and structure of your software successfully upfront, and you may also even spot extra simple methods of undertaking your goals shinier than you write the first line of code!

Comment your code liberally

If you think that your code may want an explanation, then do it. Each function needs to be preceded via 1-2 traces describing the arguments and what it returns. Comments have to inform you why you are the use of these lines. Remember to replace the remarks when you update your code!

Use regular naming conventions for variables

It will assist you to keep tune of each type of variable, and the purpose of the variable. This ability extra typing than absolutely x = a + b * c, but it will make your code an awful lot less difficult to debug and maintain. One famous convention is Hungarian notation, the place the variable name is prefixed with its type. For example, for integer variables you might use intRowCounter; strings would possibly use strUserName. It doesn't count what your naming convention is, however, be positive that it is regular and that your variable names are descriptive.

Organize your code

Use visible structures to indicate code structure. For example, indent a code block that sits inside a conditional (if, else,...) or a loop (for, while,...) Also tries inserting spaces between a variable name and an operator such as addition, subtraction, multiplication, division, and even the equal sign (myVariable = 2 + 2). As properly as making the code extra visually elegant, it makes it a good deal simpler to see the software float at a glance.

Test everything

Start via trying out every module on its own, the usage of inputs and values that you would usually expect. Then try inputs that are viable, however less common. This will flush out any hidden bugs. There is an art to test, and you will step by step construct up your capabilities with practice. Write your checks to include the following cases:

• two Extremes: Zero and past the anticipated maximum for fantastic numeric values, an empty string for text values, and null for every parameter.

• Meaningless values. Even if you don't accept as true with your cease person would input gibberish, check your software program against it anyway.

• Incorrect values. Use zero for a cost that will be used in the division, or a bad quantity when superb is anticipated or when a rectangular route will be calculated. Something that is now not a quantity when the input kind is a string, and it will be parsed for a numeric value.

Practice

The practice is an excellent alternative for gaining knowledge of the Python programming skill. There's continually something new to learn, and – perhaps more importantly – constantly something historical to relearn.

Be organized for change

Sometimes, you need to trade in your coding. You ought to be prepared for you any type of modification. Sometimes the modifications take less time. But some other aspect some exchange wants more time. So, continually you need to be equipped for any changes.

Start easy and work toward complexity.

When programming something complex, it helps to get, the less difficult constructing blocks in the area and working properly first. For example, let's say you prefer to create an evolving form on the display that follows the mouse route and adjusts the size by relying on mouse speed.

• Start by way of showing a rectangular and getting it to follow the mouse; i.e., solve motion monitoring alone, first.

• Next, make the dimension of the square relate to mouse speed; i.e., solve speed-to-shape tracking on its own.

• Finally, create the actual shapes you desire to work with and put the three aspects together.

• This strategy naturally lends itself to modular code writing, the place every aspect is in its personal self-contained block. This is very useful for code reuse (e.g. you prefer to simply use the mouse tracking in a new project), and makes for a lot less complicated debugging and maintenance.

Why You Can Use it to Improve Your Business

There are a wide variety of motives why Python is super for developing and so extensively recommended. But, it all comes back around to this simplicity and ease of use at the end of the day.

Top Software Companies Using Python

If you want some great examples of businesses that use python, for reassurance, then there are lots of choices. Almost all of the most familiar software program businesses in the world use Python. This consists of corporations such as Instagram, Amazon, Facebook, Spotify, Netflix, IBM, and even Reddit. The entire site, in this case, was all written in Python for ease of use.

It is one of the most well-known programming languages and is quickly turning into a language that is used in nearly every well-known software used on a day by day basis. For that reason, why shouldn't it be used in your corporation also?

Python Capabilities for Business

The software of the Python in your enterprise can be numerous. Often, it's a case of narrowing down what you want it to do as a substitute than surely what it can do in your business. The probabilities are endless. But, some tasks which python would excel at in your company include:

• Create an interactive consumer face for your commercial enterprise website, on the platform or app.

• Acts as on-hand supply code for a variety of resources (your website for example), as it is effortless to read.

• An excellent language for data science; such as computer learning, statistics analysis, and visualization.

• Scripting or just simply, growing a small software which automates a task.

The reality is that Python is now not solely just for developing functions, but also even for automating simple duties in your business.

What's a Python Trick?

A python trick is a shortened model of code that makes the requested characteristic to be carried out faster. A few of the tricks on hand are listed below:

Swapping values

Create a single string from all the factors in the list

Find The Most Frequent Value in A-List.

Checking if two phrases are anagrams

Reverse a String

Reverse a list

Transpose 2d array

Chained Comparison

Chained function call

Copy List

Dictionary Get

Sort Dictionary by using Value

For Else

Convert listing to comma separated

Merge Dict

Min and Max index in List

Remove duplicates from a list

Essential Tools with Python Data Analysis

After a previous couple of months, countless data science tasks in Python have launched new variations with main function updates. Some are about genuine number-crunching; others make it less difficult for Pythonistas to write quick code optimized for these jobs.

Essential Python for statistical science: SciPy 1.0

What's SciPy for?

Python customers who prefer a quick and effective math library can use NumPy, however NumPy through itself isn't very task-focused. SciPy makes use of NumPy to supply libraries for frequent math- and science-oriented programming tasks, from linear algebra to statistical work to sign processing.

How SciPy 1.0 helps with data science

SciPy has always been beneficial for supplying handy and extensively used equipment for working with math and statistics. But for the longest time, it didn't have an ideal 1.0

release, though it had sturdy backward compatibility across versions.

The set off for bringing the SciPy challenge to model 1.0, in accordance with core developer Ralf Gommers, used to be specifically a consolidation of how the mission once ran and managed. But it additionally covered a procedure for non-stop integration for the MacOS and Windows builds, as nicely as a suitable aid for prebuilt Windows binaries. This ultimate characteristic ability Windows customers can now use SciPy by not having to soar through extra hoops.

Where to obtain SciPy?

SciPy binaries can be downloaded from the Python Package Index, or via typing pip installation scipy. Source code is reachable on GitHub.

Essential Python for data science: Dask 0.15.4

What Dask is

Processing strength is more cost-effective than ever, however, it can be problematic to leverage it in the most effective, feasible way—by breaking tasks throughout more than one CPU core, different processors, or compute nodes.

Desk takes a Python job and schedules, it efficaciously throughout many systems. What's most beneficial about Dask is that the syntax used to launch Dask jobs is, in reality, the identical as the syntax used to do different matters in Python, so it requires little transforming of current code to be useful.

How Dask helps with data science

Desk gives its personal variety of some interfaces for many well-known computing device systems and scientific-computing libraries in Python. Its DataFrame object is the same as the one in the Pandas library; likewise, its Array object works simply like NumPy's. This way, you can rapidly parallelize present code via altering solely a few traces of code.

Dask can additionally be used to parallelize jobs written in pure Python and has object kinds (such as Bag) ideal for optimizing these sorts of jobs.

Where to obtain a desk?

The desk is accessible on the Python Package Index and can be set up through the pip installation disk. It's also accessible through the Anaconda distribution of Python, by way of typing Conda install disk. Source code is reachable on GitHub.

Essential Python for data science: Numba 0.35.0

What Numba is

Numba lets Python features or modules be compiled to assembly language by using the LLVM compiler framework. You can do this on the fly, every time a Python application runs, or in advance of time. In that sense, Numba is like Cython, however, Numba has been frequently extra handy to work with, though code accelerated with Cython is simpler to distribute to 0.33 parties.

How Numba helps information science

The most apparent way Numba helps statistics scientists is through increasing operations written in Python. You can prototype initiatives in pure Python, then annotate them with Numba to be more adequate for manufacturing use.

Numba can additionally grant speedups that run even quicker on hardware constructed for computer mastering and information science applications. Earlier variations of Numba supported compiling to CUDA-accelerated code, but the most recent variations sport a new, far-more-efficient GPU code reduction algorithm for faster compilation.

Numba additionally makes use of contributions from Intel, by means of the ParallelAccelerator project, to make up sure operations by routinely parallelizing them. Warning: The ParallelAccelerator additions are nevertheless experimental, so they shouldn't be used in manufacturing yet.

Where to download Numba

Numba is accessible on the Python Package Index, and it can be set up by way of typing pip set up Numba from the command line. Prebuilt binaries are accessible for Windows, MacOS, and regular Linux. It's additionally reachable as a phase of the Anaconda Python distribution, as it can be set up by means of typing Conda installation Numba. Source code is accessible on GitHub.

Essential Python for data science: Cython 0.27

What's the Purpose of Cyphone?

With Cyphone, the python code gets modified into C code which can then permit quicker runnings of magnitude. This transition is very reachable for code that is heavy in math or has loops that are tight, which is regularly seen in python when the programs are intended for machine learning, science, and engineering.

How Data Science Gets Help from Cython 0.27

The latest Cyphon version helps assist emerge as broadened for Python notebook integration. Code compiled by using Cython is adaptable for Jupyter notebooks by using way of annotations, simply like if the Cyphone is no specific than Python. As you use Cython 0.27, you are in a position to bring together the modules of Cyphon to be used for Jupyter with an optimization that is profile-guided. The modules that have this availability are optimized and gathered in accordance with data on the profile that has been generated, which will let it be quicker as it runs. Remember, the choice for this is available solely for the Cyphon whilst it is being used alongside with the GCC compiler as a guide for MSVC is no longer but established.

Where Cyphone Can Be Obtained

Cyphone can be received via Python's Package Index and is sct up by using the usage of the pip installation cython thru a command line. There are 64-bit and 32-bit binary variations handy for MacOS, familiar Linux, and Windows. The source code is available with the aid of GitHub.

HPAT Python Essentials Of Data

What is HPAT?

HPAT is Intel's High-Performance Analytics Toolkit and is an assignment that is experimental for
facts analyticsand computing device studying acceleration by using clusters. It is made up of a Python subset used to code which is parallelized robotically among clusters which makes use of the utility for Open MPI project's mpirun.

How Data Science Benefits From HPAT

Numba is the main software for HPAT, however, it does now not allow Python to be compiled, unlike it does for Cython or the project. What it does is take a subset of Python's language that is restricted, ideally, the Pandas dataframes and NumPy arrays. These make them optimized for greater than one node. Similar to Numba, the HPAT has the decorator of @jit which can seriously change more than a few functions to become their counterparts that are optimized. Additionally, it consists of an I/O module that is native which approves analyzing from HDF5 and writing to the HDF5 file.

Where Can HPAT Be Downloaded?

The availability of HPAT is solely via GitHub as a source format.

Chapter 3: How Data Analysis is Applied Today? How to Bridge Your Data Analysis with the Power of Programming? How Use it in Your Everyday Life? How to Create Dataset with Visualization? Questions and answers

All the greater critically, there isn't always one proper approach to look into the information. Contingent upon your desires and the sort of facts you gather, the right data investigation methods will move. This likewise makes it essential to see each type of information, and which strategy can bring quality outcomes. All matters considered, there are some regular approaches that come incorporated into most record examination programming given that they're powerful. These five information investigation techniques can allow you to make an increasing number of profitable and noteworthy bits of knowledge.

Quantitative and Subjective Information — What's The Distinction?

Subjective facts are marginal harder to bind in accordance with parts of an association that are gradually interpretive and abstract. This incorporates data taken from customer overviews, interviews with workers, and for the most section alludes to characteristics over amounts. All matters considered, the examination strategies utilized are much less organized than quantitative methods. Actualizing a Business Knowledge suite in your affiliation is about more than just gathering extra records — it's tied in with changing over this data into noteworthy experiences. The measure of facts an affiliation can collect nowadays from an assortment of sources provides the capacity to see in the engine, know which strategies are working, and assist groups to get prepared for future patterns. In any case, except as it should be dissected and appreciating the statistics you gather, the sum total of what you have is figures and numbers with no unique circumstance.

The preliminary phase in picking the correct records investigation system for your informational collection starts with grasp what variety of records it is — quantitative or subjective. As the name suggests, quantitative data, manage quantities and challenging numbers. This data comprises offers numbers, marketing information, for example, navigate rates, finance information, incomes, and different statistics that can be tallied and estimated dispassionately.

Estimating Quantitative Information

Quantitative examination techniques rely on the potential to precisely test and translate records established on the hard realities. Our preliminary three strategies for growing your examination sport will pay attention to quantitative information:

1. Relapse investigation

Relapse studies are terrific apparatuses when you have to make expectations and estimate future patterns. Relapses measure the connection between a reliant variable (what you want to gauge) and a free thing (the facts you use to foresee the needy variable). While you can just have one word variable, you can have an about the boundless quantity of self-sustaining ones. Relapses likewise assist you to reveal territories in your duties that can be expanded through providing patterns and connections between elements.

2. Theory tries out

Otherwise called "T Testing," this examination strategy gives you a danger to think about the information you have towards theories and suppositions you've made about your tasks. It likewise encourages you to gauge how the choices you should make will impact your association. T Testing offers you a threat to contrast two elements with discovering a connection and base preferences on the discoveries. For example, you may additionally take delivery of that extra long stretches of work are equal to greater efficiency. Prior to actualizing longer work hours, it's fundamental to guarantee there's a true association with keeping a strategic distance from a disagreeable approach.

3. Monte Carlo reenactment

As one of the most mainstream methods to compute they have an effect on of the uncommon elements on a particular factor, Monte Carlo reenactments use probability demonstrating to help foresee hazard and vulnerability. To test an idea or situation, a Monte Carlo endeavor will make use of irregular numbers and data to organize an assortment of conceivable effects to any circumstance based on any outcomes. This is amazingly useful equipment over an assortment of fields such as venture the board, money, designing, coordination, and this is solely the tip of the iceberg. By trying out an assortment of achievable outcomes, you can see how irregular factors could influence your preparations and undertakings.

4.Estimating Subjective Information

In contrast to quantitative information, subjective facts require shifting endlessly from unadulterated measurements and toward steadily summary approaches. However, you can, in any case, get rid of valuable information by utilizing, using a range of records investigation systems relying upon your requests. Our closing two techniques center around subjective information:

5. Content investigation

This method comprehends the general matters that boost in subjective information. Utilizing structures like shading coding specific topics and ideas parses literary records to detect the most broadly identified strings. Substance examinations can function admirably when managing information, for example, patron input, talk with information, open-finished reviews, and the sky is the restrict from there. This can help distinguish the greatest territories to pay attention to for development.

6. Story investigation

This sort of examination centers around the manner in which stories and ideas are imparted all through an organization and can enable you to all the more probable know the authoritative culture. This can also include deciding how representatives experience about their employments, how purchasers see an association, and how operational approaches are seen. It very properly might also be beneficial when mulling over adjustments to corporate tradition or arranging new advertising procedures.

There is no high-quality, exceptional stage for factual investigation or proper approach to do it. The technique you select ought to consistently reflect the facts you've got gathered and the kind of bits of information you want to separate. Coordinating the correct facts and investigation displays better experiences to decorate your association.

Instructions to Scaffold Your Information Investigation with the Intensity of Programming

With the quit aim for you to use it should connect you records investigation with the intensity of programming, you should first understand that information examination and writing laptop programs are no longer comparable. Here, we will talk about the key contrasts between data investigation and programming with the purpose that you can besides plenty of a stretch development between the two.

Data Analysis

Data Analysis aka Information investigation is a manner of assessing, demonstrating, cleaning, and altering records with the objective of discovering useful data, advising ends and assisting simple leadership. Information examination has several factors and methodologies, inclusive of diverse techniques beneath an assortment of names, and is utilized in a number of business, science, and sociology areas. In the current enterprise world, facts, investigation assumes a job in settling on picks step by step logical and assisting groups work all the extra viably.

Programming

PC writing PC programs are a method for giving PCs directions about what they ought to do straight away. These directions are recognized as code, and PC software engineers compose code to take care of issues or play out an undertaking.

The ultimate goal is to make something: that ought to suggest something from a website page, or a bit of programming, or even only an extraordinary picture. That is the cause PC writing laptop applications is frequently depicted as a blend among workmanship and science; it is specialized and investigative, yet innovative simultaneously.

So as the need to be obvious, the distinctions are huge. So the best route for you to join it is by means of gaining knowledge of both so you will probably make simply as read and destroy down what you made.

How to Use Information Investigation in Your Regular day to day existence?

'Goodness! This device perceives my face,' 'I earned greater earnings in light of the genuine focusing on the spotlight of this net-based life site,' 'I have a feeling of protection when I shop on the web,' 'What a precise and snappy net search tool.'

In the current cautiously upset world, we both try a lot of exercises on the web or depend on units to make our lifestyles bother free. When we are completed with our undertaking, we inspect every opportunity in adulating the innovation or the system that all-inclusive some assistance. In any case, we in most cases overlook to acclaim the groundbreaking science that receives this going – Information Science.

Here's the potential with the aid of which Information Science acts the hero in our normal everyday schedule.

Those Musical Voices

Keep in thought Jarvis from Iron Man? When you order or ask your system something, contingent upon the working association of your electronic gadget, you get the hazard to hear the beautiful voice of Siri, Cortana or Google Voice – which is in truth your personal Jarvis. The voice acknowledgment with the aid of the machine and its reaction is all workable because of information science. Controlled by means of data science, these 'voice-based partners' concentrate studying and experiences based on your voice, input/inquiry and react to supply you the ideal yield.

'Give me A chance to google It'

These are the 4 phrases that are utilized with the aid of each and every one of the men and women who stall out same region with something. Easy to articulate, would it say it isn't? All things considered, naming internet crawlers as an exemplification of brilliant innovation would not be false.

'Nonetheless, the place exactly completes a facts researcher suit into the condition?' On the off hazard that this is the concept that is rushing in your psyche, at that factor, it is important to be aware of that he is the character who fabricates solid statistics science calculations for web crawlers. Be it Google, Yippee, Bing or some other internet index, the fuse of information science calculations guarantees precise and faster outcomes.

Information Science for Business Development

You referenced 'perusing' in your 'likes' area while making your, suppose, Facebook profile. Next time you login to your record, you may see your home feed overflowing with ebook and journal advertisements. Perhaps this is your 2nd or 1/3 visit to the online life site, and you can also have not by means of any skill cherished a solitary page, but you may see every one of those advertisements.

This is on the grounds that the agencies enlisted on the stage are using records investigation and actually focusing on highlights to draw in attainable customers who have premium, enthusiasm or preferences that are identified with the item or administration that they are selling. The more facts the website online has, the better it receives with its focusing on.

Like the Manner in which You Fly

Did you realize that there are more than a few service experts co-ops working at a misfortune? Either because of low inhabitance, high gas fee or low taxes (to draw clients). There are numerous carriers – all-around – fighting due to the fact of these elements.

In any case, few of these aircraft have begun making use of Information Science to carry their accounting file makes the experience of the section. The other reasons carriers too:

1 Choose which classification of Airbus to purchase

2 Whether to stop in the middle of or straightforwardly arrive at the goal

3 Dispatch new as properly as deal with the contemporary steadfastness packages for the customers

This is possible simply because of Information Science. Aircraft accumulate and crunch facts from a previous time and settle on higher options for the future to wind up gainful.

So each time you get a shabby flight ticket, you recognize who is in charge of it.

It Gives You a Validity Identification

Specific corporations in India supply believability critiques to firms and people. FICO rating is one such model. Anyway, how would you discern they do it?

At the factor when a statistical researcher sends the systems of data science in this specific circumstance, it helps in mining information, for example, a person's or company's profiling, past consumption, and one of a kind element that further help with examining the hazard of default. In this manner, based totally on statistics obtained via Information Science, the groups give a ranking to the elements. Next time your credit score receives affirmed, thank your information.

Information Science: Running in the Veins of the Advanced World

Be it coordinations or self-driving vehicles, Information Science are all over the place. In light of its developing magnitude and degree, many are settling on commercial enterprise investigation and data science confirmation courses. Information Science is changing the world, and on the off hazard that you are lively about this interesting control, at that point this is definitely a chance to take a crack at a records science path, and satisfy your myth of getting to be data researcher and notably affect each day lives of an exceptional many folks around the world.

Instructions to Make Dataset with Visualization

You can make statistics units by means of making use of Data Visualization record sets.

In Data Visualization, you can transfer data from an assortment of sources (for instance, spreadsheets, CSV documents,

Combination Applications, and several databases) to your framework, and investigate your statistics to discover connections, locate examples, and see patterns.

When you wreck down a big association of records and discover huge patterns in your data, you can seize these statistics in Data Visualization, and import these record sets in BI Distributer. You can make use of the facts units from Data Visualization to make reports, distribute reviews (on the net or to numerous goals), plan reports, and burst reports.

You cannot make use of Data Visualization data sets of Essbase data as a source.

To make records set through using a piece of information sent from Data Visualization:

1.   On the partial sheet of the data mannequin proofreader, select DataSet and pick out DV Data Sets.

The Data Sets tab documents each one of the facts sets you made in Data Visualization.

2.   In the Data Sets tab, select the data set you need to use for pixel-immaculate detailing.

3.   Click Next.

4.   Enter a name for the records set.

5.   If you want to organize parameters, play out these means for each and every parameter:

a.   Click Include Parameter.

b.   Select a part from the Segment Name list.

c.   If you want to exchange the identity of the parameter, alter the name in the Parameter field.

6.   Click Completion.

After you import a data set that is planned in Data Visualization, on the off hazard that you change the shape of the records set in Data Visualization, you must physically alter and invigorate the information set in BI Distributer. You cannot import the articulations and patron decided aspects from Data

Visualization to a BI Distributed data mannequin and you can't join between record sets.

Make a Data Set Utilizing a Data Visualization Data Stream

You can utilize the Data Visualization information streams to make statistics sets.

The accompanying information streams don't seem to be bolstered:

- Data streams made with the Spare Model choice.

- Data streams with stretched data sets.

To make an information set to use Data Visualization information streams:

1. Select Data Sets, click on New Data Set in the Graph tab, and after that pick out DV Data Sets.

2. Click the Data Streams tab.

3.   Select a data stream you want to make use of and click Straightaway.

4.   Enter an identity for the facts set.

5.   If you need to arrange parameters, play out these skills for each parameter:

a.   Click Include Parameter.

b.   Select a section from the Segment Name list.

c.   If you need to trace the name of the parameter, alter the title in the Parameter field.

6.   Click Completion

Questions and Answers

Python Confirmation is the most appeared for after understanding in programming space. In this section, you will become familiar with the most asked questions related to Python. These questions are the one asset from where you can support your assembly planning. There are 100 questions on

Python Programming necessities which will assist you with a number of mastery levels to obtain the greatest information available.

Essential Python Questions and Answers

Q1. What is the biggest difference among rundown lists and tuples in Python?

Rundown versus TUPLES

LIST TUPLES

Records are alterable i.e they can be edited. Tuples are changeless (tuples are documents which cannot be altered).

Records are extra slow than tuples.   Tuples are quicker than run down.

Sentence structure: list_1 = [10, 'Chelsea', 20] Syntax: tup_1 = (10, 'Chelsea', 20)

Q2. What are the key highlights of Python?

•	Python is a deciphered language. That implies that no longer at all like dialects like C and its variants, Python mustn't be arranged before it is run. Other translated dialects include PHP and Ruby.

•	Python is powerfully composed, this implies you don't have to specify the kinds of elements when you proclaim them or anything like that. You can do things like x=111 and later on x="I'm a string" except mistake

•	Python is terrific to article orientated programming in that it allows that means of classes alongside piece and legacy. Python does no longer strategy specifiers (like C++'s open, private).

•	In Python, capacities are the pinnacle of the line objects. This implies they can be relegated to factors, came returned from different capacities and go into capacities. Classes are moreover 5 famous person objects

•   Writing Python code is fast, but running it is regularly extra more sluggish than aggregated dialects. Fortunately, Python lets in the consideration of C based augmentations, so bottlenecks can be upgraded away and often are. The Numpy bundle is an authentic case of this present, it's sincerely very quick on the grounds that a terrific deal on the calculating it does isn't always clearly performed through Python

•   Python discovers us in several circles – net applications, mechanization, logical demonstrating, substantial facts purposes and some more. It's moreover regularly utilized as a "stick" code to get extraordinary dialects and components to get along.

Q3. What kind of language is python? Programming or scripting?

Ans: Python is in shape for scripting, but as a rule sense, it is regarded as a universally beneficial programming language. To discover out about Scripting, you can allude to the Python Scripting Instructional exercise.

Q4.How is Python a translated language?

Ans: A translated language is any programming language which isn't in the desktop stage code earlier than runtime. Along these lines, Python is a translated language.

Q5.What is kick 8?

Ans: Kick represents Python Improvement Proposition. It is a lot of ideas that decide how to organize Python code for most severe lucidness.

Q6. How is memory overseen in Python?

Ans:

1.   Memory administration in python is overseen via Python personal storage space. All Python items and statistics structures are located in a private stack. The software program

engineer does no longer approach this non-public load. The python mediator deals with this.

2.   The undertaking of a pile area for Python articles is finished with the aid of Python's memory administrator. The middle Programming interface affords to get right of entry to sure apparatuses for the software program engineer to code.

3.   Python likewise has a built-in town worker, which reuses all the unused memory accordingly that it very well may also be made reachable to the pile space.

Q7. What is namespace in Python?

Ans: A namespace is a naming framework used to ensure that names are one of a sort to abstain from naming clashes.

Q8. What is PYTHONPATH?

Ans: It is a scenario variable which is utilized when a module is imported. At something pointy, a module is imported, PYTHONPATH is likewise admired test for the nearness of the imported modules in extraordinary indexes. The translator makes use of it to discern out which module to stack.

Q9. What are python modules? Name some typically utilized implicit modules in Python?

Ans: Python modules are documents containing Python code. This code can both be capacities classes or factors. A Python module is a .py report containing executable code.

A component of the typically utilized implicit modules is:

- os

- sys

- math

- random

- data time

- JSON

Q10.What are the local factors and worldwide factors in Python?

Worldwide Factors:

Factors announced outside a potential or in the global house are referred to as worldwide factors. These elements can be gotten to by way of any culpability in the program.

Local Factors: Any factor proclaimed inside a capability are recognized as a close-by the factor. This variable is accessible in the nearby space and now not in the international space.

Q11. Is python case touchy?

Ans: Yes. Python is a case touchy language.

Q12.What is type alternate in Python?

Ans: Type transformation alludes to the exchange of one record type into another.

Int () – changes over any statistics kind into entire range shot

coast() – adjustments over any statistics kind into buoy type

ord() – modifications over characters into an entire wide variety

hex() – adjustments over entire numbers to hexadecimal

oct() – changes over the complete variety to octal

tuple() – This ability is utilized to exchange over to a tuple.

set() – This capacity restores the sort subsequent to altering over to set.

list() – This capability is utilized to alternate over any data kind of a rundown type.

dict() – This potential is utilized to exchange over a tuple of request (key,value) into a word reference.

Str () – Used to trade over entire wide variable into a string.

complex(real,imag) – This functionconverts actual numbers to complex(real,imag) number.

Q13. How to introduce Python on Windows and set way faster?

Ans: To introduce Python on Windows, pursue the under steps:

• Install python from this connection:

https://www.python.org/downloads/

• After this, introduce it on your PC. Search for the location where PYTHON has been added on your PC using the accompanying order on your course brief: cmd python.

• Then go to slicing part framework settings and include another variable and identify it as PYTHON_NAME and glue the replicated way.

• Look for the way factor, pick its worth and pick out 'alter'.

• Add a semicolon towards the section of the association on the off risk that it's absent and, at that factor type %PYTHON_HOME%

Q14. Is the space required in python?

Ans: Space is vital for Python. It determines a rectangular of code. All code inside circles, classes, capacities, and so on are determined inside an indented square. It is usually finished utilizing 4 area characters. On the off hazard that your code isn't indented essences, it may not execute exactly and will toss error also.

Q15. What is the distinction between Python Exhibits and records?

Ans: Clusters and records, in Python, have a comparable approach for placing away information. In any case, clusters can hold simply a solitary statistics type elements, although archives can hold any facts kind components.

Q16. What are works in Python?

Ans: A capability is rectangular of code which is achieved simply when it is called. To characterize a Python work, the def watchword is utilized.

Q17.What is __init__?

Ans: __init__ is a strategy or constructor in Python. This technique is naturally known to distribute memory when every other article/occurrence of a category is made. All training has the __init__ strategy.

Q18.What is lambda work?

Ans: An unknown capability is known as lambda work. This potential can have any quantity of parameters in any case, can have solely one proclamation.

Q19. What is self in Python?

Ans: Self is a case or an object of a class. In Python, this is expressly blanketed as an important parameter. Nonetheless, this is not the state of affairs in Java the place it's discretionary. It separates between the techniques and characteristics of a type with nearby factors.

The self variable in the unit approach has alluded to the recently made object while in special strategies, it alludes to the article whose strategy was once called.

Q20. How does break, proceed and pass work?

Break Allows circle to stop when some situation is met and the control is moved to the following articulation.

Continue   Allows avoiding some piece of a circle when some specific situation is met and the manipulate is moved to the start of the circle

Pass   Used when you need some rectangular of code, grammatically, then again, you need to skirt its execution. This is in truth an invalid activity. Nothing takes place when this is executed.

Q21. What does [::- 1} do?

Ans: [::- 1] is utilized to flip around the request for a show-off or a succession.

For instance:

1

2

3 import cluster as arr

My_Array=arr.array('i',[1,2,3,4,5])

My_Array[::- 1]

Yield: array('i', [5, 4, 3, 2, 1])

[:: - 1] reprints a switched replica of requests statistics structures, for example, a showcase or a rundown. the first cluster or rundown stays unaltered.

Q22. How may you randomize the matters of a rundown set up in Python?

Ans: Consider the mannequin tested as follows:

1

2

3

4   from irregular import mix

x = ['Keep', 'The', 'Blue', 'Banner', 'Flying', 'High']

shuffle(x)

print(x)

The yield of the accompanying code is as beneath.

['Flying', 'Keep', 'Blue', 'High', 'The', 'Flag']

Q23. What are python iterators?

Ans: Iterators are objects which can be crossed on the other hand or iterated upon.

Q24. How do you produce arbitrary numbers in Python?

Ans: Irregular module is the general module that is utilized to create an arbitrary number. The technique is characterized as:

1

2   imports irregular

random.random

The announcement is random.random() method return the coasting factor number that is in the scope of [0, 1). The capability produces irregular buoy numbers. The techniques that are utilized with the arbitrary classification are the bound techniques for the shrouded occurrences. The instances of the Arbitrary should be possible to demonstrate the multi-stringing packages that make an alternate case of parsing strings. The different arbitrary mills that are utilized in this area:

1.   randrange(a, b): it selections a complete number and characterize the variation in the center of [a, b). It restores the

aspects of choosing it haphazardly from the range that is determined. It doesn't construct a range object.

2.   uniform(a, b): it selections a skimming factor wide variety that is characterized in the scope of [a,b].Iyt restores the drifting factor wide variety

3.   normalvariate(mean, sdev): it is utilized for the ordinary conveyance the place the mu is a imply and the sdev is a sigma that is utilized for well-known deviation.

4.   The Irregular classification that is utilized and instantiated makes a free numerous arbitrary quantity generator.

Q25. What is the difference between variable and xrange?

Ans: Generally, xrange and range are exactly identical concerning usefulness. The two of them provide a strategy to create a rundown of numbers for you to utilize, anyway you please. The essential distinction is that range restores a Python rundown object and x vary restores an xrange object.

This implies xrange would not truly create a static rundown at run-time like very does. It makes the qualities as you want them with a wonderful technique referred to as the yield. This technique is utilized with a form of an object known as generators. That implies that on the off threat that you have an extraordinarily massive vary you'd like to create a rundown for, kingdom one billion, xrange is the capability to utilize.

This is in particular legitimate on the off chance that you have an extraordinary memory delicate framework, for example, a cellphone that you are working with, as vary will use as much memory as it can to make your variety of complete numbers, which can bring about a Memory Blunder and crash your program. It's a memory hungry brute.

Q26. How would you compose remarks in python?

Ans: Remarks in Python start with a # character. Be that as it may, on the other hand on occasion, remarking is finished making use of docstrings(strings encased interior triple statements).

Model:

#Comments in Python begin this way

print("Comments in Python start with a #")

Yield: Remarks in Python commencement with a #

Q27. What is pickling and unpickling?

Ans: Pickle module acknowledges any Python article and changes over it into a string portrayal and dumps it into a file via utilizing dump work, this procedure is referred to as pickling. While the way towards recuperating unique Python objects from the put-away string portrayal is known as unpickling.

Q28. What are the generators in python?

Ans: Capacities that arrival an iterable association of matters are known as generators.

Q29. By what capability will you underwrite the foremost letter of string?

Ans: In Python, the underwrite() approach underwrites the fundamental letter of a string. On the off danger that the string as of now contains a capital letter towards the start, at that point, it restores the first string.

Q30. In what capacity will you convert a string to all lowercase?

Ans: To change over a string to lowercase, lower() capability can be utilized.

Model:

1

2   stg='ABCD'

```
print(stg.lower())
```

Yield: abcd

Q31. How to comment on more than a few lines in python?

Ans: Multi-line remarks come up with other than one line. Every one of the lines to be remarked is to be prefixed by way of a #. You can likewise a normally splendid effortless route technique to commentary several lines. You have to virtually maintain the Ctrl key and left snap in every spot any place you need to include a # character and type a # simply once. This will remark each and every one of the streams where you presented your cursor.

Q32. What's the use of docstrings for in Python?

Ans: Docstrings are not actually remarks, be that as it may, they are strings of documentations. These docstrings are within triple statements. They are never doled out to anything and along these lines, now and again, work nicely for the motivation in the back of remarks as.

Q33. What is the motivation of this in administrators?

Ans: Administrators are exotic capacities. They take at least one trait and produce an equivalent result.

is: returns genuine when 2 operands are valid (Model: "a" will be 'a')

not: restores the reverse of the boolean worth

in: tests if some factor is accessible in some succession

Q34. What is the use of assistance() and dir() work in Python?

Ans: Help() and dir() the two capacities are open from the Python mediator and utilized for survey a solidified dump of inherent capacities.

1.   Help() work: The assistance() work is utilized to show the documentation string and furthermore encourages you to see the assistance recognized with modules, watchwords, characteristics, and so on.

2.   Dir() work: The dir() work is utilized to show the characterized images.

Q35. At something point Python exits, for what reason isn't always all the reminiscence de-distributed?

Ans:

1.   Whenever Python exits, in particular, these Python modules which are having round references to extraordinary items or the articles that are referenced from the global namespaces are now not generally de-allotted or liberated.

2.   It is challenging to de-dispense these parts of memory that are held by the C library.

3.   On exit, in view of having its personal wonderful tidy up the system, Python would try to de-apportion/annihilate each other article.

Q36. What is a word reference in Python?

Ans: The implicit datatypes in Python is known as word reference. It characterizes coordinated connection amongst keys and qualities. Word references comprise a pair of keys and their comparing esteems. Word references are filed by way of keys.

How about we take a model:

The accompanying mannequin includes some keys. Nation, Capital, and PM. Their comparing esteems are India, Delhi, and Modi individually.

1   dict={'Country':'India','Capital':'Delhi','PM':'Modi'}

1   print dict[Country]

India

1   print dict[Capital]

97

Delhi

```
1      print dict[PM]
```

Modi

Q37. By what technique can the ternary administrators be utilized in python?

Ans: The Ternary administrator is the administrator that is utilized to show the restrictive proclamations. This includes real or false traits with an explanation that should be assessed for it.

Linguistic structure:

The Ternary administrator will be given as:

[on_true] if [expression] else [on_false]x, y = 25, 50big = x if x < y else y

Model:

The articulation gets assessed like in the match that x

Q38. What are negative files and for what cause would they say they are utilized?

Ans: The preparations in Python are recorded and it involves the positive just as pure numbers. The numbers that are positive utilizations '0' that is made use of as first listing and '1' as the subsequent file and the procedure goes on like that.

The file for the terrible variant starts from '- 1' that speaks to the final document of the succession and '- 2' as the penultimate listing and the grouping conveys ahead like the tremendous number.

The bad list is utilized to expel any new-line areas from the string and allow the string to with the exception of the last character that is given as S[:- 1]. The poor list is likewise used to reveal the record to communicate to the string in proper request.

Q39. What are Python bundles?

Ans: Python bundles are namespaces containing numerous modules.

Q40.How can files be erased in Python?

Ans: To erase a document in Python, you have to import the operating system Module. From that factor forward, you have to utilize the os.remove() work.

Model:

```
1

2     import os

os.remove("xyz.txt")
```

Q41. What are worked in the kinds of python?

Ans: Worked in varieties in Python are as per the following –

• Integers

- Floating-point

- Complex numbers

- Strings

- Boolean

- Built-in capacities

Q42. What preferences do NumPy clusters provide over (settled) Python records?

Ans:

1.   Python's rundowns are educated universally useful compartments. They aid (genuinely) fine inclusion, erasure, adding, and link, and Python's rundown appreciations make them simple to construct and control.

2.   They have sure confinements: they do not bolster "vectorized" duties like elementwise expansion and increase,

and the way that they can include objects of varying sorts suggest that Python ought to save typing data for every component, and have to execute type dispatching code when working on each component.

3.   NumPy isn't simply gradually effective; it is additionally increasingly helpful. You get a top-notch deal of vector and lattice tasks for nothing, which once in a while allow one to hold away from superfluous work. Furthermore, they are moreover proficiently actualized.

4.   NumPy showcase is quicker and you get a high-quality deal worked in with NumPy, FFTs, convolutions, rapid looking, necessary measurements, straight variable based totally math, histograms, and so forth.

Q43. How to add esteems to a python exhibit?

Ans: Components can be brought to a cluster, utilizing the add(), expand() and the complement (i,x) capacities.

Model:

```
1

2

3

4

5

6

7       a=arr.array('d', [1.1 , 2.1 ,3.1] )

a.append(3.4)

print(a)

a.extend([4.5,6.3,6.8])

print(a)

a.insert(2,3.8)

print(a
```

Yield:

array('d', [1.1, 2.1, 3.1, 3.4])

array('d', [1.1, 2.1, 3.1, 3.4, 4.5, 6.3, 6.8])

array('d', [1.1, 2.1, 3.8, 3.1, 3.4, 4.5, 6.3, 6.8])

Q44. How to expel esteems to a python exhibit?

Ans: Cluster factors can be expelled utilizing pop () or evacuate () technique. The distinction between these two capacities is that the preceding returns the erased really worthwhile the remaining does not.

Model:

1

2

3

4

```
5       a=arr.array('d', [1.1, 2.2, 3.8, 3.1, 3.7, 1.2, 4.6])
```

print(a.pop())

print(a.pop(3))

a.remove(1.1)

print(a)

Yield:

4.6

3.1

array('d', [2.2, 3.8, 3.7, 1.2])

Q45. Does Python have Uh oh ideas?

Ans: Python is an object located programming language. This implies any software can be understood in python by way of making an article model. Be that as it may, Python can be dealt with as procedural just as fundamental language.

Q46. What is the difference between profound and shallow duplicate?

Ans: Shallow duplicate is utilized when every other case type gets made and it maintains the traits that are replicated in the new example. Shallow reproduction is utilized to reproducing the reference pointers sincerely like it duplicates the qualities. These references factor to the first articles and the progressions made in any man or woman from the classification will likewise have an effect on its first duplicate. Shallow reproduction lets in faster execution of the software and it relies upon the size of the statistics that is utilized.

Profound reproduction is utilized to save the features that are as of now replicated. The profound replica does not reproduce the reference pointers to the items. It makes the reference to an item and the news article that is printed with the aid of any other article gets put away. The progressions made in the first replica may not influence whatever other reproduction that uses the item. Profound replica makes the execution of the application greater sluggish due to the fact of making certain duplicates for every article that is being called.

Q47. How is Multithreading performed in Python?

Ans:

1.   Python has a multi-stringing bundle, then again on the off hazard that you want to multi-string to speed your code up, at that factor, it is typically no longer a clever concept to make use of it.

2.   Python has a strengthen known as the Worldwide Mediator Lock (GIL). The GIL ensures that simply one of your 'strings' can execute at any one time. A string gets the GIL, completes a little work, at that factor passes the GIL onto the following string.

3.   This happens in all respects swiftly so to the human eye it may appear as though your strings are executed in parallel, but they are extremely actually alternating making use of a similar CPU center.

4.   All this GIL passing adds overhead to execution. This implies on the off risk that you want to make your code run quicker, at that point using the stringing bundle often is genuinely now not a clever thought.

Q48. What is the procedure of assemblage and connecting in python?

Ans: The accumulating and connecting enables the new expansions to be arranged appropriately with no mistake and the connecting should be possible just when it passes the ordered system. On the off chance that the dynamic stacking is utilized, at that point, it relies upon the style that is being furnished with the framework. The python translator can be utilized to give the dynamic stacking of the arrangement documents and will reconstruct the mediator.

The means that are required in this as:

1.   Create a record with any name and in any language that is upheld by the compiler of your framework. For instance file.c or file.cpp

2.   Place this document in the Modules/registry of the dispersion which is getting utilized.

3.   Add a line in the document Setup.local that is available in the Modules/registry.

4.   Run the document utilizing spam file.o

5.   After a fruitful, keep running of this modify the mediator by utilizing the make order on the top-level catalog.

6.   If the record is changed at that point run rebuildMakefile by utilizing the order as 'make Makefile'.

Q49. What are the Python libraries? Name a couple of them.

Python libraries are an accumulation of Python bundles. A portion of the significantly utilized python libraries is – Numpy, Pandas, Matplotlib, Scikit-learn and some more.

Q50. What is partly utilized for?

The split() technique is utilized to isolate a given string in Python.

Q51. How to import modules in python?

Modules can be imported utilizing the import catchphrase. You can import modules in three different ways-

Uh oh Inquiries, questions

Q52. Clarify Legacy in Python with a model.

Ans: Legacy enables One class to increase all the members(say traits and strategies) of another class. Legacy gives code reusability, makes it simpler to make and keep up an application. The class from which we are acquiring is considered super-class and the class that is acquired is known as an inferred/tyke class.

They are various kinds of legacy upheld by Python:

1. Single Legacy – where a determined class secures the individuals from a solitary superclass.

2. Multilevel legacy – a determined class d1 in acquiring from base class base1, and d2 are acquired from base2.

3. Hierarchical legacy – from one base class you can acquire any number of youngster classes

4. Multiple legacies – a got class is acquired from more than one base class.

Q53. How are classes made in Python?

Ans: Class in Python is made utilizing the class catchphrase.

Model:

```
1

2

3

4

5       class Worker:

def __init__(self, name):

self.name = name

E1=Employee("abc")

print(E1.name)

Yield: abc
```

Q54. What is monkey fixing in Python?

Ans: In Python, the term monkey fix just alludes to dynamic adjustments of a class or module at run-time.

Q55. Does python bolster various legacies?

Ans: Numerous legacy implies that a class can be gotten from more than one parent classes. Python supports various legacies, in contrast to Java.

Q56. What is Polymorphism in Python?

Ans: Polymorphism implies the capacity to take numerous structures. In this way, for example, in the event that the parent class has a strategy named ABC, at that point the youngster class additionally can have a technique with a similar name ABC having its very own parameters and factors. Python permits polymorphism.

Q57. Characterize embodiment in Python?

Ans: Embodiment means restricting the code and the information together. A Python class in the case of exemplification.

Q58. How would you do information reflection in Python?

Ans: Information Deliberation is giving just the required subtleties and concealing the execution from the world. It tends to be accomplished in Python by utilizing interfaces and theoretical classes.

Q59.Does python utilize to get to specifiers?

Ans: Python does not deny access to an occurrence variable or capacity. Python sets out the idea of prefixing the name of the variable, capacity or technique with a solitary or twofold underscores to mimic the conduct of secured and private access specifiers.

Q60. How to make a vacant class in Python?

Ans: A vacant class is a class that does not have any code characterized inside its square. It tends to be made utilizing the pass catchphrase. Be that as it may, you can make objects of this class outside the class itself. IN PYTHON THE PASS direction does nothing when its executed. It's an invalid explanation.

Q61. What does an article() do?

Ans: It restores a featureless article that is a base for all classes. Likewise, it doesn't take any parameters.

Essential Python Projects

Q62. Compose a program in Python to create Star triangle.

1

2

3

4   def pyfunc(r):

for x in range(r):

print(' '*(r-x-1)+'*'*(2*x+1))

pyfunc(9)

Yield:

*

***

*****

****

****

****

****

****

****

Q63. Compose a program to create a Fibonacci arrangement in Python.

1

2

3

4

5

6

7

8

9

10

11

12

13

14   # Enter number of terms needed   #0,1,1,2,3,5....

a=int(input("Enter the terms"))

f=0   #first component of arrangement

s=1   #second component of arrangement

in the event that a<=0:

  print("The mentioned arrangement is

```
",f)

else:

  print(f,s,end=" ")

  for x in range(2,a):

      next=f+s                           

      print(next,end=" ")

      f=s

      s=next</pre>
```

Q64. Compose a program in Python to check if a number is prime.

1

2

3

4

5

6

7

8

9

10   a=int(input("enter number"))

in the event that a>1:

  for x in range(2,a):

      if(a%x)==0:

          print("not prime")

          break

  else:

      print("Prime")

else:

  print("not prime")

Q69. Compose a program in Python to check if an arrangement is a Palindrome.

1

2

3

4

5

6   a=input("enter grouping")

b=a[::- 1]

in the event that a==b:

  print("palindrome")

else:

  print("Not a Palindrome")

Q65. Compose a joke that will tally the number of capital letters in a record. Your code should work regardless of whether the document is too huge to fit in memory.

Ans: Let us initially compose a numerous line arrangement and after that convert it to joke code.

1

2

3

4

5

6   with open(SOME_LARGE_FILE) as fh:

```
tally = 0

content = fh.read()

for character in content:

on the off chance that character.isupper():

tally += 1
```

We will presently attempt to change this into a solitary line.

```
1    count sum(1 for line in fh for character in line if character.isupper())
```

Q66. Compose an arranging calculation for a numerical dataset in Python.

Ans: The accompanying code can be utilized to sort a rundown in Python:

```
1

2
```

3

4   list = ["1", "4", "0", "6", "9"]

list = [int(i) for I in list]

list.sort()

print (list)

Q67. Taking a gander at the beneath code, record the last estimations of A0, A1,

Ans.

1

2

3

4

5

6

7   A0 = dict(zip(('a','b','c','d','e'),(1,2,3,4,5)))

A1 = range(10)A2 = sorted([i for I in A1 on the off chance that I in A0])

A3 = sorted([A0[s] for s in A0])

A4 = [i for I in A1 on the off chance that I in A3]

A5 = {i:i*i for I in A1}

A6 = [[i,i*i] for I in A1]

print(A0,A1,A2,A3,A4,A5,A6)

Ans: The accompanying will be the last yields of A0, A1, ... A6

A0 − {'a': 1, 'c': 3, 'b': 2, 'e': 5, 'd': 4} # the request may change

A1 = range(0, 10)

A2 = []

A3 = [1, 2, 3, 4, 5]

A4 = [1, 2, 3, 4, 5]

A5 = {0: 0, 1: 1, 2: 4, 3: 9, 4: 16, 5: 25, 6: 36, 7: 49, 8: 64, 9: 81}

A6 = [[0, 0], [1, 1], [2, 4], [3, 9], [4, 16], [5, 25], [6, 36], [7, 49], [8, 64], [9, 81]]

Python Libraries Inquiries, Questions

Q68. Clarify what Carafe is and its advantages?

Ans: Carafe is a net microframework for Python structured on "Werkzeug, Jinja2 and honest goals" BSD permit. Werkzeug and Jinja2 are two of their conditions. This implies it will have practically zero conditions on outside libraries. It makes the structure light while there is little reliance to refresh and fewer protection bugs.

A session in actuality permits you to recollect information starting with one solicitation then onto the next. In a flagon, a session makes use of a marked deal with so the customer can take a gander at the session substance and alter. The consumer

can alter the session if it just has the mystery key
Flask.secret_key.

Q69. Is Django most appropriate to Carafe?

Ans: Django and Flagon map the URL's or addresses composed
in the internet browsers to capacities in Python.

The flagon is a lot extra easier contrasted with Django in any
case, Carafe does not whole a ton for you that means you should
indicate the subtleties, whilst Django completes
an extraordinary deal for you wherein you would not have to do
plenty work. Django comprises of prewritten code, which the
patron must smash down whilst Cup gives the customers to
make their very personal code, thusly, making it less challenging
to recognize the code. Actually, both are in a similar way super
and both include their very own blessings and disadvantages.

Q70. Notice the contrasts between Django, Pyramid, and Carafe.

Ans:

• Flask is a "micro framework" if truth be told work for a little utility with much less complicated necessities. In flagon, you need to utilize outer libraries. The jar is prepared to utilize.

• The pyramid is labored for bigger applications. It offers adaptability and offers the fashion designer a risk to make use of the correct gadgets for their venture. The dressmaker can pick the database, URL structure, templating fashion and the sky is the restriction from there. The pyramid is tremendously configurable.

• Django can likewise be utilized for higher functions simply like a Pyramid. It incorporates an ORM.

Q71. Talk about Django engineering.

Ans: Django MVT Example:

The clothier gives the Model, the view and the layout, then just maps it to a URL and Django does the enchantment serve it to the client.

Q72. Clarify how you can set up the Database in Django.

Ans: You can make use of the order alter mysite/setting.py, it is a regular python module with module degree talking to Django settings.

Django makes use of SQLite as a count of course; it is easy for Django customers with that ability it might not require any different sort of establishment. For the situation, your database choice is unique that you have to the accompanying keys in the DATABASE 'default' factor to coordinate your database association settings.

• Engines: you can trade the database via using 'django.db.backends.sqlite3' , 'django.db.backeneds.mysql', 'django.db.backends.postgresql_psycopg2', 'django.db.backcnds.oraclc, and many othcrs

• Name: The name of your database. In the scenario in the tournament that you are utilizing SQLite as your database, all things considered, the database will be a record on your PC,

Name ought to be a full outright way, including the reported identity of that document.

• If you are now not picking SQLite as your database, then settings like Secret Pharaohs, Host, Client, and so forth ought to be included.

Django makes use of SQLite as a default database, it stores information as a solitary file in the filesystem. On the off chance that you do have a database server—PostgreSQL, MySQL, Prophet, MSSQL—and need to make use of it as hostile to SQLite, at that point make use of your database's corporation units to make another database for your Django venture. In any case, with your (vacant) database set up, all that final components is to disclose to Django how to utilize it. This is the place your venture's settings.py document comes in.

We will encompass the accompanying strains of code to the setting.py document:

1

2

3

4

5

6 DATABASES = {

'default': {

'Motor' : 'django.db.backends.sqlite3',

'NAME' : os.path.join(BASE_DIR, 'db.sqlite3'),

}

}

Q73. Give a model of how you can compose a VIEW in Django?

Ans: This is the potential via which we can utilize compose a view in Django:

1

2

3

4

5

6

7 from django.http import HttpResponse

import datetime

def Current_datetime(request):

presently = datetime.datetime.now()

html = "It is nowadays %s p.c now

return HttpResponse(html)

Returns the present date and time, as an HTML report

Q74. Notice what the Django layouts comprise of.

Ans: The format is a simple content material record. It can make any content, material primarily based arrangement like XML, CSV, HTML, and so forth. A plan consists of factors that get supplanted with qualities when the format is assessed and labels (% tag %) that manipulate the purpose of the layout.

Q75. Clarify the utilization of session in Django structure?

Ans: Django gives a session that approves you to store and get better data on a for each site-guest premise. Django abstracts the way towards sending and getting treats, through setting a session ID to treat on the customer side and putting away all the associated records on the server-side.

So the statistics itself aren't always put away client side. This is nice from a protection viewpoint.

Q76. Rundown out the legacy patterns in Django.

Ans: In Django, there are three viable legacy styles:

1. Abstract Base Classes: This style is utilized when you just need

parent's classification to preserve information that you would opt for now not to compose for each and every tyke model.

2. Multi-table Legacy: This style is utilized On the off threat that you are sub-classing a modern-day mannequin and need every mannequin to have its very personal database table.

3. Proxy models: You can make use of this model, On the off threat that you just need to alter the Python level conduct of the model, except altering the model's fields.

Web Scratching – Python Inquiries, Questions

Q77. How to Spare A Picture Locally Utilizing Python Whose URL Address I Definitely Know?

Ans: We will make use of the accompanying code to spare a photograph locally from a URL tackle

1

2 import urllib.request

urllib.request.urlretrieve("URL", "nearby filename.jpg")

Q78. How would possibly you Get the Google reserve age of any URL or website page?

Ans: Utilize the accompanying URL design:

http://webcache.googleusercontent.com/search?q=cache:URLG OESHERE

Make sure to supplant "URLGOESHERE" with the quality, viable web address of the web page or internet site whose reserve you need to recover and see the best probability for. For instance, to take a look at the Google Webcache duration of edureka.co you'd utilize the accompanying URL:

http://webcache.googleusercontent.com/search?q=cache:edure ka.co

Q79. You are required to scrap facts from IMDb top 250 movies page. It ought to just have fields

action image name, year, and rating.

Ans: We will utilize the accompanying strains of code:

1

2

3

4

5

6

7

8

9

10

11

12

13

14

15

16

17

```
18
19 from bs4 import BeautifulSoup

import needs

import sys

url = 'http://www.imdb.com/graph/top'

reaction = requests.get(url)

soup = BeautifulSoup(response.text)

tr = soup.findChildren("tr")

tr = iter(tr)

next(tr)

for action photograph in tr:

title = movie.find('td', {'class':

'titleColumn'} ).find('a').contents[0]

year = movie.find('td', {'class': 'titleColumn'} ).find('span',

{'class': 'secondaryInfo'}).contents[0]

rating = movie.find('td', {'class':

'ratingColumn imdbRating'} ).find('strong').contents[0]

push = title + ' - ' + yr + ' + ' + rating

print(row)
```

The above code will help scrap data from IMDb's major 250

rundown

Information Investigation – Python Inquiries, Questions

Q80. What is guiding work in Python?

Ans: map ability executes the capacity given as the foremost
competition in each and every one of the aspects of
the iterable allowed as the subsequent contention. On the off
risk that the ability given takes in greater than 1 contention, at
that point several iterables are given. #Follow the connection to
comprehend increasingly comparative capacities.

Q81. Is python numpy superior to records?

Ans: We use the python numpy cluster as an alternative than a
rundown in light of the following three reasons:

1. Less Memory

2. Fast

3. Convenient

For extra information on these parameters, you can allude to
this location – Numpy Versus Rundown list.

Q82. How to get records of N most severe qualities in a NumPy exhibit?

Ans: We can get the files of N biggest features in a NumPy to show off utilizing the code beneath:

1

2

3 import numpy as np

arr = np.array([1, 3, 2, 4, 5])

print(arr.argsort()[-3:][::- 1])

Yield

[4 3 1]

Q83. How would you compute percentiles with Python/NumPy?

Ans: We can compute percentiles with the accompanying code

1

2

3

```
4 import numpy as np

a = np.array([1,2,3,4,5])

p = np.percentile(a, 50) #Returns fiftieth percentile, for instance
center

print(p)

Yield
```

Q84. What is the contrast between NumPy and SciPy?

Ans:

1. In a perfect world, NumPy would include only the showcase data type and the most critical activities: ordering, arranging, reshaping, fundamental elementwise capacities, and so forth.

2. All numerical code would stay in SciPy. In any case, one of NumPy's significant goals is a similarity, so Numpy attempts to hold all highlights upheld by means of both of its forerunners.

3. Thus NumPy contains some direct variable primarily based

math capacities, regardless of the reality that these all the greater correctly have a place in SciPy. Regardless, SciPy contains all the extra absolutely blanketed diversifications of the direct variable based math modules, just as several different numerical calculations.

4. If you are doing logical registering with python, you ought to most probably introduce both NumPy and SciPy. Most new highlights have a region in SciPy as opposed to NumPy.

Q85. How would you make 3D plots/perceptions, making use of NumPy/SciPy?

Ans: Like 2D plotting, 3D designs is previous the extent of NumPy and SciPy, alternatively in a similar way as in the 2D case, bundles exist that comprise with NumPy. Matplotlib offers necessary 3D plotting in the mplot3d subpackage, even though Mayavi offers an extensive scope of pinnacle notch 3D perception highlights, using the great VTK motor.

Various Decision Questions (MCQ)

Q86. Which of the accompanying explanations makes a lexicon? (Various Right Answers Conceivable)

a) d = {}

b) d = {"john":40, "peter":45}

c) d = {40:"john", 45:"peter"}

d) d = (40:"john", 45:"50")

Answer: b, c, and d.

Word references are made by means of determining keys and values.

Q87. Which one of these is floor division?

a)/

b)/

c) %

d) None of the referenced

Answer: b)/

At the factor when each of the operands is wide variety then python hacks at the portion phase and offers you the round off worth, to find the unique solution use, flooring division. For ex, 5/2 = 2.5, however, each of the operands is complete quantity so answer of this articulation in python is 2. To locate the 2.5 as the solution, use ground division utilizing/. Along these lines, 5//2 = 2.5

Q88. What is the best plausible length of an identifier?

a) 31 characters

b) sixty three characters

c) seventy nine characters

d) Nothing from what was mentioned just once

Answer: d) Nothing from what was simply stated Identifiers can be of any length.

Q89. For what cause is neighborhood variable names starting with an underscore debilitated?

a) they are utilized to exhibit non-public elements of a classification

b) they befuddle the mediator

c) they are utilized to exhibit international elements

d) they avert execution

Answer: a) they are utilized to display a private variable of a class

As Python has no perception of private factors, riding underscores are utilized to exhibit factors that have until now not be gotten to from outdoor the class.

Q90. Which of coming up subsequent is an invalid articulation?

an) abc = 1,000,000

b) a b c = a thousand 2000 3000

c) a,b,c = 1000, 2000, 3000

d) a_b_c = 1,000,000

Answer: b) a b c = one thousand 2000 3000

Spaces are now not authorized in component names.

Q91. What is the yield of the accompanying?

1

2

3

4

5

6

7 try:

on the off danger that '1' != 1:

raise "someError"

else:

print("someError has not occured")

with the exception of "someError":

print ("someError has occured")

a) someError has occurred

b) someError has not occurred

c) invalid code

d) Nothing, unless there are other picks

Answer: c) invalid code

Another distinctive case category must acquire from a

BaseException. There is no such legacy here.

Q92. Assume list1 is [2, 33, 222, 14, 25], What is list1[-1] ?

a) Blunder

b) None

c) 25

d) 2

Answer: c) 25

The listing - 1 relates to the remaining file in the rundown.

Q93. To open a report c:scores.txt for composing, we use

an) outfile = open("c:scores.txt", "r")

b) outfile = open("c:scores.txt", "w")

c) outfile = open(file = "c:scores.txt", "r")

d) outfile = open(file = "c:scores.txt", "o")

Answer: b) The region contains twofold cuts ( ) and w is utilized to exhibit that file is being composed to.

Q94. What is the yield of the accompanying?

1

2

3

4

5

6

7

8 f = None

for I in range (5):

with open("data.txt", "w") as f:

on the off hazard that I > 2:

break

print f.closed

a) Genuine

b) False

c) None

d) Mistake

Answer: a) Genuine

The WITH clarification when utilized to open record ensures that the document article is shut when the with square exits.

Q95. When will the else section of striving with the exception of else be executed?

a) consistently

b) when an exclusive case takes place

c) when no special case happens

d) when a different case occurs into apart from rectangular

Answer: c) when no specific case takes place

The else part is executed when no different case happens.

Chapter 4: What is Numpy? A Beginner's Look of Numpy with Data Analysis, How Numpy Is Used with Python, What is Panda? A Panda Introduction Using Data Analysis, The Use of Panda with Python

NumPy is the key bundle for logical registering in Python. It is a Python library that offers a multidimensional showcase object, unique inferred objects, (for example, veiled clusters and grids), and a grouping of schedules for rapid tasks on clusters, consisting of numerical, coherent, structure control, arranging, choosing, I/O, discrete Fourier changes, quintessential straight variable based math, indispensable factual activities, irregular reenactment and substantially more.

At the center of the NumPy bundle, is the ndarray object. This exemplifies n-dimensional varieties of homogeneous information types, with numerous activities being carried out in assembling code for execution. There are a few significant contrasts between NumPy well-known shows and the popular Python groupings:

• NumPy clusters have a constant measurement at creation, distinctive to Python documents (which can advance progressive). Changing the measurement of a ndarray will make some other exhibit and erase the first.

• The aspects in a NumPy cluster are altogether required to be of comparable data type, and in consequence will be a comparative dimension in memory. The unique case: one can have the sorts of (Python, inclusive of NumPy) objects, alongside these strains taking into account sorts of quite a number estimated components.

• NumPy reveals encourage stepped forward numerical and one of a kind kinds of things to do on massive portions of information. Ordinarily, such duties are carried out more productively and with much less code than is conceivable utilizing Python's worked in successions.

• Creating lots of logical and scientific Python-based bundles are making use of NumPy exhibits; however these in most cases bolsters Python-succession input, they convert such contribution to NumPy clusters earlier than preparing, and they frequently yield NumPy clusters. At the end of the day, so as to efficaciously utilize a great deal (maybe even most) of the present logical/scientific Python-based programming, truely realizing how to make use of Python's labored in succession kinds is missing - one likewise has to realize how to utilize NumPy exhibits.

The focus on grouping size and velocity are particularly widespread in logical registering. As a fundamental model, consider the instance of growing each and every aspect in a 1-D grouping with the referring to issue in another succession of a comparable length. In the match that the statistics are put away in two Python records, an and b, we should emphasize over each component:

This creates the proper answer, but on the off chance that an and b each comprise a massive number of numbers, we will pay the price for the wasteful elements of circling in Python. We ought to reap a comparable assignment substantially extra swiftly in C by means of composing (for lucidity we disregard variable displays and instatements, memory designation, and so forth.)

This spares all the overhead engaged with interpreting the Python code and controlling Python objects, yet to the detriment of the advantages picked up from coding in Python. Moreover, the coding work required increments with the dimensionality of our information. On account of a 2-D cluster, for instance, the C code (abbreviated as in the past) grows to NumPy offers us the quality of the two universes: thing by-component things to do are the "default mode" when an ndarray is included, but the aspect by-component undertaking is swiftly carried out with the aid of pre-gathered C code. In NumPy

```
c = a * b
```

Does what the preceding fashions do, at shut C speeds, but with the code effortlessness we count on from something dependent on Python. Surely, the NumPy phrase is lots less complex! This last mannequin represents two of NumPy's highlights which are the premise of a lot of its capacity: vectorization and broadcasting.

Vectorization depicts the non appearance of any unequivocal circling, ordering, and so forth., in the code - these matters are occurring, obviously, honestly "in the background" in advanced, pre-incorporated C code. Vectorized code has numerous preferences, among which are:

• vectorized code is steadily brief and less difficult to peruse

• fewer lines of code for the most section implies fewer bugs

• the code all the extra closely takes after well-known numerical documentation (making it simpler, commonly, to precise code scientific develops)

• vectorization brings about greater "Pythonic" code. Without vectorization, our code would be covered with wasteful and tough to peruse for circles.

Broadcasting is the term used to depict the sore issue by-component behavior of activities; for the most section talking, in NumPy all tasks, wide variety juggling tasks, yet coherent, piece shrewd, utilitarian, and so forth., elevate on in this verifiable factor by-component design, i.e., they communicate. Besides, in the model over, an and bought to be multidimensional types of a comparable shape, or a scalar and an exhibit, or even two sorts of with a variety of shapes, gave that the little cluster is "expandable" to the kingdom of the higher so that the subsequent talk is unambiguous. For factor by way of point "rules" of broadcasting see numpy.doc.broadcasting.

NumPy definitely bolsters an article situated methodology, beginning, by and by, with ndarray. For instance, ndarray is a class, having more than a few strategies and qualities. A big variety of its techniques replicate works in the exterior most NumPy namespace, giving the software engineer whole possibility to code in whichever worldview she likes as nicely as which seems to be most fitting to the job that wants to be done.

A Prologue to Numpy Utilizing Information Examination

When you've got delivered NumPy you can import it as a library:

import numpy as np

Numpy has many worked in capacities and abilities. We may not cover them the entirety besides instead we will concentrate on in all likelihood the most tremendous parts of Numpy: clusters (vectors, lattices), and quantity age. How about we begin by using inspecting clusters.

Numpy Exhibits

NumPy well-knownshows are the precept way we will utilize Numpy all via the course. Numpy clusters basically come in two flavors: vectors and networks. Vectors are cautiously 1-d famous and frameworks are 2-d (however you must take note of a grid can at existing have simply one line or one section).

How about we begin our acquaintance with the aid of investigating how to make NumPy clusters.

Making NumPy Exhibits

From a Python Rundown

We can make a cluster by means of straightforwardly changing over a rundown or rundown of records

One good-sized visible cue here: At something factor, you need to utilize a bundle's potential you use package_abbreviation.function documentation. (Ex.: np.array())

package_abbreviation originates from how you imported the bundle (for example 'import numpy as np')

```
np.array(my_list)
```

```
array([1, 2, 3])
```

```
my_matrix = [[1,2,3],[4,5,6],[7,8,9]]
```

```
my_matrix
```

```
[[1, 2, 3], [4, 5, 6], [7, 8, 9]]
```

```
np.array(my_matrix)
```

```
array([[1, 2, 3],
```

```
[4, 5, 6],
```

```
[7, 8, 9]])
```

Worked in Capacities in NumPy to create Exhibits

There are bunches of labored in methods to produce Exhibits

arange

Fundamentally the equal as a range () work, np. arrange (start (inclusive), stop (excluding), advance)) work returns equitably dispersed features inside a given interim.

```
np.arange(0,10)
```

```
array([0, 1, 2, 3, 4, 5, 6, 7, 8, 9])
```

np.arange(0,11,2)

array([0, 2, 4, 6, 8, 10])

zeros and ones

To produce varieties of zeros or ones: np.zeros(shape of the grid composed in as a tuple (lines, segments), np.ones(shape of the network composed in as a tuple). At the point when just a single rivalry is given, makes a vector. – > array(1,2,31,2,3).shape - (3,)

np.zeros(3)

array([0., 0., 0.])

np.zeros((5,5))

array([[0., 0., 0., 0., 0.],

[0., 0., 0., 0., 0.],

[0., 0., 0., 0., 0.],

[0., 0., 0., 0., 0.],

[0., 0., 0., 0., 0.]])

np.ones(3)

array([1., 1., 1.])

np.ones((3,3))

array([[1., 1., 1.],

[1., 1., 1.],

[1., 1., 1.]])

linspace

Returns equitably dispersed numbers over a predefined

interim. np.linspace(start, stop, number of numbers to be

returned). Notice that stop is comprehensive here.

np.linspace(0,10,3)

array([0., 5., 10.])

np.linspace(0,10,50)

array([0 , 0.20408163, 0.40816327, 0.6122449 ,

0.81632653, 1.02040816, 1.2244898 , 1.42857143,

1.63265306, 1.83673469, 2.04081633, 2.24489796,

2.44897959, 2.65306122, 2.85714286, 3.06122449,

3.26530612, 3.46938776, 3.67346939, 3.87755102,

4.08163265, 4.28571429, 4.48979592, 4.69387755,

4.89795918, 5.10204082, 5.30612245, 5.51020408,

5.71428571, 5.91836735, 6.12244898, 6.32653061,

6.53061224, 6.73469388, 6.93877551, 7.14285714,

7.34693878, 7.55102041, 7.75510204, 7.95918367,

8.16326531, 8.36734694, 8.57142857, 8.7755102 ,

8.97959184, 9.18367347, 9.3877551 , 9.59183673,

9.79591837, 10.])

eye

Makes a personality lattice. Accepting you comprehend what is
a character and framework. Generally seem to be at it its
utilization.

np.eye(4)

array([[1., 0., 0., 0.],

[0., 1., 0., 0.],

[0., 0., 1., 0.],

[0., 0., 0., 1.]])

Producing Irregular Number Exhibits

Numpy likewise has hundreds of techniques to make irregular

number exhibits. Remember to type in no. random first when utilizing an irregular number producing capacities! It is a common slip-up you will do when you begin coding.

np.random.rand()

Makes a variety of the given shape and populate it with arbitrary examples from a uniform dispersion over [0, 1). On the off threat that no rivalry is given, makes a solitary boy

np.random.rand(2)

array([0.11570539, 0.35279769])
np.random.rand(5,5)
array([[0.66660768, 0.87589888, 0.12421056, 0.65074126, 0.60260888],
[0.70027668, 0.85572434, 0.8464595 , 0.2735416 , 0.10955384],
[0.0670566 , 0.83267738, 0.9082729 , 0.58249129, 0.12305748],

[0.27948423, 0.66422017, 0.95639833, 0.34238788,

0.9578872],

[0.72155386, 0.3035422 , 0.85249683, 0.30414307,

0.79718816]])

np.random.randn()

Returns an example (or tests) from the "standard typical"

appropriation. Dissimilar to rand which is uniform:

np.random.randn(2)

array([-0.27954018, 0.90078368])

np.random.randn(5,5)

array([[0.70154515, 0.22441999, 1.33563186, 0.82872577, -

0.28247509],

[0.64489788, 0.61815094, - 0.81693168, - 0.30102424, -

0.29030574],

[0.8695976 , 0.413755 , 2.20047208, 0.17955692, -

0.82159344],

[0.59264235, 1.29869894, - 1.18870241, 0.11590888, -

0.09181687],

[-0.96924265, - 1.62888685, - 2.05787102, - 0.29705576,

0.68915542]])

np.random.randint()

Returns irregular whole numbers from low (comprehensive) to

excessive (selective).

np.random.randint(1,100)

44

np.random.randint(1,100,10)

array([99, 75, 46, 34, 5, 24, 60, 10, 44, 20])

Exhibit Traits and Techniques

How about we talk about some precious traits and strategies or a

cluster. Beneath two clusters made with np.arange()

and np.random.randint().

arr = np.arange(25)

ranarr = np.random.randint(0,50,10)

arr

array([0, 1, 2, 3, 4, 5, 6, 7, 8, 9, 10, 11, 12, 13, 14, 15, 16,

17, 18, 19, 20, 21, 22, 23, 24])

ranarr

array([10, 12, 41, 17, 49, 2, 46, 3, 19, 39])

Reshape

With .reshape() approach you can restore an exhibit containing similar records with some other shape. Underneath the one dimensional arr cluster is reshaped to 5 traces and 5 segments two dimensional network. Significant visual cue here: When you apply techniques to the articles (numpy gadgets or one-of-a-kind articles that numpy can work with) you don't have to kind in 'np.' documentation any more. (ie. arr is an show off article and numpy's reshape() approach can be kept walking without 'np.')

arr.reshape(5,5)

```
array([[ 0,          1,          2,          3,          4],
       [ 5,          6,          7,          8,          9],
       [10,         11,         12,         13,         14],
       [15,         16,         17,         18,         19],
       [20,         21,         22,         23,         24]])
```

max(),min(),argmax(),argmin()

These are helpful strategies for discovering max or min esteems in the exhibits. To find out their document areas uses argmin and argmax.

ranarr

```
array([10, 12, 41, 17, 49, 2, 46, 3, 19, 39])
```
ranarr.max()

49

ranarr.argmax()

4

ranarr.min()

2

ranarr.argmin()

5

Qualities : Shape

shape demonstrates the structure fantastic of clusters. Properties are no longer strategies. Notice there are no paranthesis () on them.

Vector

arr.shape

(25,)

# Notice the two preparations of sections
arr.reshape(1,25)
array([[0, 1, 2, 3, 4, 5, 6, 7, 8, 9, 10, 11, 12, 13, 14, 15, 16, 17, 18, 19, 20, 21, 22, 23, 24]])
arr.reshape(1,25).shape

(1, 25)

arr.reshape(25,1)
array([[0],

[1],

[2],

[3],

[4],

[5],

[6],

[7],

[8],

[9],

[10],

[11],

[12],

[13],

[14],

[15],

[16],

[17],

[18],

[19],

[20],

[21],

[22],

[23],

[24]])

arr.reshape(25,1).shape

(25,   1)

Traits : dtype

dtype demonstrates the records kind of the article in the exhibit. Notice it is not quite the equal as the sort() work. type() work demonstrates the kind of the item. – >type(arr) would return numpy.ndarray.

arr.dtype

dtype('int64')

Very tons done Now you have performed the important Segment of the NumPy! Have a destroy presently, perhaps snatch an espresso or something, earlier than proceeding. :)

2 - NumPy Ordering and Determination

In this session we will identify how to choose elements or gatherings of components from an exhibit.

```
# We need to make an example cluster

arr = np.arange(0,11)
#Show                                                    it
arr
array([ 0,   1,   2,   3,   4,   5,   6,   7,   8,   9,   10])
```

Section   Ordering   and   Choice

This is the easiest approach to pick one or a few elements of an exhibit. It's fundamentally the same as python records:

#Getting   an   incentive   at   a   document

arr[8]

8

#Getting values in a range mannequin

arr[1:5]

array([1, 2, 3, 4])

#Get values in a variable mannequin 2

arr[0:5]

array([0, 1, 2, 3, 4])

Broadcasting

This is a huge component. Not at all like Python records, NumPy

clusters can communicate:

#Setting an incentive with file run (Broadcasting)

arr[0:5]=100

#Show

arr

array([100, 100, 100, 100, 100, 5, 6, 7, 8, 9, 10])

Presently, once more it is necessary to consider that Python won't duplicate the rundowns or clusters when you explicitly would no longer funny story about this. On the off danger that you make changes on a reduction of a cluster, the progressions will be connected to the first rundown as well.

Reset cluster, we will see why I wanted to reset in a minute

arr = np.arange(0,11)

#Show

arr

array([0, 1, 2, 3, 4, 5, 6, 7, 8, 9, 10])

#Important notes on Cuts

slice_of_arr = arr[0:6]

#Show cut

slice_of_arr
array([0, 1, 2, 3, 4, 5])

#Change Cut

slice_of_arr[:]=99

#Show Cut once more

slice_of_arr
array([99, 99, 99, 99, 99, 99])

Presently word the progressions likewise show up in our special exhibit!

arr

array([99, 99, 99, 99, 99, 99, 6, 7, 8, 9, 10])

Information isn't replicated, it's a perspective on the first exhibit! This evades memory issues!

```
#To get a duplicate, be specific
arr_copy = arr.copy()
arr_copy
array([99, 99, 99, 99, 99, 99, 6, 7, 8, 9, 10])
```

Ordering a 2D exhibit (networks)

The custom configuration is arr_2drowrowcolcolor arr_2drow,colrow,col. The subsequent strategy is increasingly more every day to see. In any case, it is your taste how to file at any charge

```
arr_2d = np.array(([5,10,15],[20,25,30],[35,40,45]))
```

```
#Show
arr_2d
array([[ 5, 10, 15],
[20, 25, 30],
[35, 40, 45]])


#Indexing line


arr_2d[1]
array([20, 25, 30])


# Arrangement is arr_2d[row][col] or arr_2d[row,col]


# Getting singular component esteems first Strategy


arr_2d[1][0]
20


# Getting singular element esteems second Strategy
```

arr_2d[1,0]

20

2D show off slicing

#This will get every one of the aspects of ordered 0 push and recorded 1 push and from the listed 1 segment for the remainder of the segments.

arr_2d[:2,1:]
array([[10, 15],

[25, 30]])

#This will get the filed 2 push.

arr_2d[2]
array([35, 40, 45])

#This will alo get the recorded 2 push.

```
arr_2d[2,:]
array([35, 40, 45])
```

Extravagant Ordering

Extravagant ordering enables you to select total lines or sections out of order,to show this current, we unexpectedly work out a Numpy exhibit:

```
#Set up the lattice
arr2d = np.zeros((10,10))


#Length of show off


arr_length = arr2d.shape[1]


#Set up show off


for I in range(arr_length):
```

```
arr2d[i] = I
arr2d
array([[0., 0., 0., 0., 0., 0., 0., 0., 0., 0.],
[1., 1., 1., 1., 1., 1., 1., 1., 1., 1.],
[2., 2., 2., 2., 2., 2., 2., 2., 2., 2.],
[3., 3., 3., 3., 3., 3., 3., 3., 3., 3.],
[4., 4., 4., 4., 4., 4., 4., 4., 4., 4.],
[5., 5., 5., 5., 5., 5., 5., 5., 5., 5.],
[6., 6., 6., 6., 6., 6., 6., 6., 6., 6.],
[7., 7., 7., 7., 7., 7., 7., 7., 7., 7.],
[8., 8., 8., 8., 8., 8., 8., 8., 8., 8.],
[9., 9., 9., 9., 9., 9., 9., 9., 9., 9.]])
```

Extravagant ordering approves the accompanying

```
arr2d[[2,4,6,8]]
array([[2., 2., 2., 2., 2., 2., 2., 2., 2., 2.],
[4., 4., 4., 4., 4., 4., 4., 4., 4., 4.],
[6., 6., 6., 6., 6., 6., 6., 6., 6., 6.],
[8., 8., 8., 8., 8., 8., 8., 8., 8., 8.]])
```

#Allows in any request

arr2d[[6,4,2,7]]

array([[6., 6., 6., 6., 6., 6., 6., 6., 6., 6.],

[4., 4., 4., 4., 4., 4., 4., 4., 4., 4.],

[2., 2., 2., 2., 2., 2., 2., 2., 2., 2.],

[7., 7., 7., 7., 7., 7., 7., 7., 7., 7.]])

Somewhat outside assistance isn't always destructive.

Ordering a 2nd grid can be somewhat confounding from the outset, in particular when you begin to consist of step size. Attempt google photograph looking NumPy ordering to discover treasured images

Choice

Above we talked about how we can pick elements from NumPy exhibits with ordering. How about we rapidly go over how making use of sections for desire established on correlation administrators.

```
arr = np.arange(1,11)

arr

array([ 1, 2, 3, 4, 5, 6, 7, 8, 9, 10])
```

With NumPy clusters tasks with correlation administrators makes varieties of boolean qualities. Keep in thought This may not work with records. What's more, with NumPy clusters we can even do contingent desire making use of this element.

```
arr > four

array([False, False, False, False, Genuine, Genuine, Genuine,
Genuine, Genuine,
True])

bool_arr = arr>4

bool_arr
```

array([False, False, False, False, Genuine, Genuine, Genuine, Genuine, Genuine,

True])

arr[bool_arr]

array([5, 6, 7, 8, 9, 10])

arr[arr>2]

array([3, 4, 5, 6, 7, 8, 9, 10])

x = 2

arr[arr>x]

array([3, 4, 5, 6, 7, 8, 9, 10])

All round done! Choice and Ordering is ridiculously significant. I can no longer prescribe greater to rehearse on this... Prepared? How about we go the remaining session of NumPy.

3 - NumPy Activities

Math

Math activities with lattices would by no means been simpler! How about we see a few models:

```
arr = np.arange(0,10)

arr + arr

array([ 0, 2, 4, 6, 8, 10, 12, 14, 16, 18])

arr * arr

array([ 0, 1, 4, 9, 16, 25, 36, 49, 64, 81])

arr - arr

array([0, 0, 0, 0, 0, 0, 0, 0, 0, 0])


# Another first rate factor of Numpy: NumPy will give you a
word on division by zero, then again not a blunder!


# Just supplanted with nan


arr/arr


C:\ProgramData\Anaconda3\lib\site-
packages\ipykernel_launcher.py:3: RuntimeWarning: invalid
well worth skilled in true_divide
```

This is discrete from the ipykernel bundle so we can abstain from doing imports till

array([nan, 1., 1., 1., 1., 1., 1., 1., 1., 1.])

Getting a be aware not a blunder strategy likewise applies to number/0. NumPy will yield endless.

1/arr

C:\ProgramData\Anaconda3\lib\site-packages\ipykernel_launcher.py:2: RuntimeWarning: partition by zero experienced in true_divide
array([inf, 1. , 0.5 , 0.33333333, 0.25 ,
0.2 , 0.16666667, 0.14285714, 0.125 , 0.11111111])
arr**3
array([0, 1, 8, 27, 64, 125, 216, 343, 512, 729], dtype=int32)

All inclusive Cluster Capacities

In spite of the reality that NumPy is certainly no longer a logical estimation library, it accompanies numerous all inclusive cluster capacities, which are basically certain numerical activities you can use to play out the activity over the exhibit. How about we reveal some ordinary ones:

#Taking Square Roots

np.sqrt(arr)

array([0. , 1. , 1.41421356, 1.73205081, 2. ,

2.23606798, 2.44948974, 2.64575131, 2.82842712, three])

#Calculating exponential (e^)

np.exp(arr)

array([1.00000000e+00, 2.71828183e+00, 7.38905610e+00,

2.00855369e+01,

5.45981500e+01, 1.48413159e+02, 4.03428793e+02,

1.09663316e+03,

2.98095799e+03, 8.10308393e+03])

```
np.max(arr) #same as arr.max()
9
np.sin(arr)
array([ 0 , 0.84147098, 0.90929743, 0.14112001, - 0.7568025 ,
- 0.95892427, - 0.2794155 , 0.6569866 , 0.98935825,
0.41211849])
np.log(arr)
```

C:\ProgramData\Anaconda3\lib\site-packages\ipykernel_launcher.py:1: RuntimeWarning: partition by zero skilled in log

"""Section factor for propelling an IPython bit.

```
array([ - inf, 0 , 0.69314718, 1.09861229, 1.38629436,
1.60943791, 1.79175947, 1.94591015, 2.07944154, 2.19722458])
```

How C

an Numpy Be Used with Python

Exhibit in Numpy is a desk of components (typically numbers), the majority of a comparable sort, filed via a tuple of wonderful entire numbers. In Numpy, number of measurements of the cluster is called rank of the array.A tuple of total numbers giving the measurement of the show off alongside every dimension is regarded as state of the exhibit. A cluster classification in Numpy is known as as ndarray. Components in Numpy clusters are gotten to through using rectangular sections and can be brought by means of using settled Python Records.

Making a Numpy Cluster

Clusters in Numpy can be made by means of numerous ways, with one-of-a-kind variety of Positions, characterizing the measurement of the Exhibit. Clusters can likewise be made with the utilization of unique information types, for example, records, tuples, and so forth. The sort of the resultant exhibit is derived from the variety of the components in the groupings.

Note: Sort of show off can be expressly characterised while

making the cluster.

```python
# Python application for

# Formation of Clusters

import numpy as np

# Making a rank 1 Cluster

arr = np.array([1, 2, 3])

print("Array with Rank 1: \n",arr)

# Making a rank 2 Cluster

arr = np.array([[1, 2, 3],
[4, 5, 6]])
print("Array with Rank 2: \n", arr)
```

Making a cluster from tuple

```
arr = np.array((1, 3, 2))
print("\nArray made utilizing "
"passed tuple:\n", arr)
```

Keep strolling on IDE

Yield:

Cluster with Rank 1:

[1 2 3]

Cluster with Rank 2:

[[1 2 3]
[4 5 6]]

Cluster made utilizing surpassed tuple:

[1 three 2]

Getting to the cluster Record

In a numpy cluster, ordering or getting to the showcase file ought to be viable in several ways. To print a scope of a cluster, cutting is finished. Cutting of a variable in another show off, whichry in another show off which is utilized to print a scope of components from the first cluster. Since, reduce exhibit holds a scope of aspects of the first cluster, altering content material with the assistance of reduce showcase adjusts the first exhibit content.

Python program to illustrate

ordering in numpy cluster

import numpy as np

Beginning Cluster

```python
arr = np.array([[-1, 2, 0, 4],

[4, - 0.5, 6, 0],

[2.6, 0, 7, 8],

[3, - 7, 4, 2.0]])
print("Initial Cluster: ")
print(arr)


# Printing a scope of Cluster


# with the utilization of slicing approach


sliced_arr = arr[:2, ::2]
print ("Cluster with initial 2 traces and"
" interchange columns(0 and 2):\n", sliced_arr)


# Printing aspects at


# explicit Records
```

Index_arr = arr[[1, 1, 0, 3],

[3, 2, 1, 0]]

print ("\nElements at information (1, 3), "

"(1, 2), (0, 1), (3, 0):\n", Index_arr)

Keep running on IDE

Yield:

Beginning Exhibit:

[[-1. 2. 0 4]

[four - 0.5 6. zero]

[2.6 0 7. eight]

[3 - 7. 4 2.]]

Exhibit with preliminary 2 lines and interchange columns(0 and 2):

[[-1. 0.]

[4 6.]]

Components at lists (1, 3), (1, 2), (0, 1), (3, 0):

[0 54 2. 3.]

Essential Cluster Tasks

In numpy, clusters allow a wide scope of activities which can be performed on a precise exhibit or a combo of Clusters. These exercise comprise some imperative Numerical exercise simply as Unary and Double tasks.

Python software to illustrate

necessary things to do on single exhibit

import numpy as np

```python
# Characterizing Exhibit 1

a = np.array([[1, 2],
[3, 4]])

# Characterizing Exhibit 2

b = np.array([[4, 3],
[2, 1]])

# Adding 1 to every factor

print ("Adding 1 to each component:", a + 1)

# Subtracting 2 from each issue

print ("\nSubtracting 2 from each component:", b - 2)

# aggregate of cluster elements
```

Performing Unary tasks

print ("\nSum of all show off "

"components: ", a.sum())

Including two exhibits

Performing Paired things to do

print ("\nArray sum:\n", a + b)

Keep jogging on IDE

Yield:

Adding 1 to each component:

[[2 3]
[4 5]]

Subtracting 2 from every component:

[[2 1]

[zero - 1]]

Entirety of all cluster components: 10

Exhibit whole:

[[5 5]

[5 5]]

More on Numpy Exhibits

• Basic Exhibit Activities in Numpy

• Advanced Exhibit Activities in Numpy

• Basic Cutting and Propelled Ordering in NumPy Python

Information Types in Numpy

Each Numpy exhibit is a desk of aspects (typically numbers), the majority of a comparable kind, listed by a tuple of fantastic complete numbers. Each ndarray has a related data type (dtype) object. This records kind object (dtype) gives data about the layout of the cluster. The estimations of a ndarrwhich can be thought of as a touching rectangular of memory bytes rectangular of memory bytes which can be translated through the dtype object. Numpy gives a massive assocthat can be utilize the season of the Cluster Christian season of Cluster creatione season of Cluster creation, Numpy tries to parent a datatype, then again works that build famous more frequently than now not likewise include a discretionary rivalry to unequivocally decide the datatype.

Building a Datatype Item

In Numpy, datatypes of Clusters want no longer to be characterised besides if a precise datatype is required. Numpy tries to pare whichcharacterized, besidesn the construcdata type.constructor work.

Python Program to make

```python
# an information kind object
import numpy as np
# Number datatype
# speculated by Numpy
x = np.array([1, 2])


print("Integer Datatype: ")
print(x.dtype)
# Buoy datatype
# speculated through Numpy
x = np.array([1.0, 2.0])
print("\nFloat Datatype: ")
print(x.dtype)
# Constrained Datatype
x = np.array([1, 2], dtype = np.int64)
print("\nForcing a Datatype: ")
print(x.dtype)
```

Keep running on IDE

Yield:

Whole number Datatype:

int64

Buoy Datatype:

float64

Compelling a Datatype:

int64

Math Activities on DataType cluster

In Numpy clusters, imperative scientific tasks are performed element astute on the exhibit. These activities are connected each as administrator over-burdens and as capacities. Numerous treasured capacities are given in Numpy to performing calculations on Clusters, for example, entirety: for growth of Exhibit components, T: for Transpose of components, and so on.

Python Program to make

an records kind object

```python
import numpy as np

# First Cluster

arr1 = np.array([[4, 7], [2, 6]],

dtype = np.float64)

# Second Cluster

arr2 = np.array([[3, 6], [2, 8]],
dtype = np.float64)

# Expansion of two Clusters

Whole = np.add(arr1, arr2)
print("Addition of Two Clusters: ")
print(Sum)

# Expansion of all Cluster aspects
```

```python
# making use of predefined total strategy

Sum1 = np.sum(arr1)
print("\nAddition of Cluster components: ")
print(Sum1)


# Square base of Cluster

Sqrt = np.sqrt(arr1)

print("\nSquare base of Array1 components: ")
print(Sqrt)


# Transpose of Cluster

# utilising In-constructed work 'T'

Trans_arr = arr1.T
print("\nTranspose of Exhibit: ")
print(Trans_arr)
```

Keep running on IDE

Yield:

Expansion of Two Exhibits:

[[7. 13.]

[4 14.]]

Expansion of Exhibit components:

19.0

Square basis of Array1 components:

[[2. 2.64575131]

[1.41421356 2.44948974]]

Transpose of Exhibit:

[[4. 2.]

[7. 6.]]

What is Pamda?

Pandas means "Python Information Investigation Library". As indicated by the Wikipedia page on Pandas, "the name is gotten from the expression "board information", an econometrics term for multidimensional prepared informational indexes." Yet I consider it's only a charming name to a superPandas are a considerable distinct benefit

onsiderable distinct benefit with regards to dissecting facts with Python and it is one of the most appreciated and typically utilized devices in data munging/wrangling if now not Tilized one. Pandas is an open source, allowed to use (under a BSD permit) and it used to be originally composed with the aid of Wes McKinney (here's a connare

about Pandas is that it takes statistics (like a CSV or TSV document, or a SQL database) and makes a Python object with lines and segments known as data outline that looks basically the same as desk in a measurable programming (think Exceed expectations or SPSS for instance. Individuals who be aware of about R would see likenesses to R as well). This

is such an exquisite amount of easier to work with in contrast with working with records and moreover lexicons thru for circles or rundown understanding (if it is not too an awful lot trouble do not hesitate to look at one of my previous weblog postsabout essential statistics examination using Python. It would have been such a splendid amount of easier to do what I did there utilizing Pandas!).

Establishment and Beginning

So as to "get" Pandas you would need to introduce it. You would likewise need Python 2.7 or more as a pre-necessity for establishment. It is moreover reliant on exceptional libraries (like Numpy) and has discretionary dependancies (like Matplotlib for plotting). In this way, I feel that the most undemanding method to get Pandas set up is to introduce it via a bundle like the Boa constrictor circulation, "a move stage dissemination for facts investigation and logical figuring." There you can down load the Windows, working gadget X and Linux adaptations. In the tournament that you need to introduce in an alternate manner, these are the full institution guidelines.

So as to make use of Pandas in your Python IDE (Coordinated Improvement Condition) like Jupyter Scratch pad or Spyder (them two accompany Boa constrictor as a depend of course), you have to import the Pandas library first. Bringing in a library capacity stacking it into the memory and later on it is there for you to work with. So as to import Pandas you need to truly run the accompanying code:

```
import pandas as pd
import numpy as np
```

Typicalequent section ('as pd') so you can get to Pandas with 'pd.command' alternatively than waiting for to compose 'pandas.command' every time you have to make use of it. Additionally, you would import numpy also, on the grounds that it is extraordinarily treasured library for logical figuring with Python. Presently Pandas is prepared for use! Keep in mind, you would need to do it each time you commence any other Jupyter Scratch pad, Spyder document and so on.

Working with Pandas
Stacking and Sparing Information with Pandas

When you want to utilize Pandas for record examination, you may for the most section use it in one of three unique ways:

• Convert a Python's rundown, phrase reference or Numpy showcase to a Pandas data define

• Open a close by document utilizing Pandas, more frequently than no longer a CSV document, alternatively, could likewise be a delimited content material document (like TSV), Exceed expectations, and so forth

• Open a far flung report or database like a CSV or a JSONon a website thru a URL or study from a SQL table/database

There are more than a few directions to every one of these choices, but when you open a document, they would resemble this:

pd.read_filetype()

As referenced before, there are unique report types Pandas can work with, so you would supplant "document type" with the genuine, well, document type (like CSV). You would provide the way, file name and so on internal the enclosure. Inside the bracket you can likewise omit a number of contentions that become aware of with how to open the document. There is a range of contentions and so as to be aware of all you them, you would need to peruse the documentation for instance, the documentation for pd.read_csv() would contain every one of the contentions you can go in this Pandas direction.

So as to exchange over a specific Python object (lexicon, documents and so forth) the essential route is:

pd.DataFrame()

Inside the enclosure you would decide the object(s) you're making the facts outline from. This order likewise has a variety of contentions (interactive connection).

You can likewise spare a records side you're working with/on to quite a number types of files (like CSV, Exceed expectations, JSON and SQL tables). The familiar code for that is:

df.to_filetype(filename)

Survey and Assessing Information

Since you've got stacked your information, it's an ideal probability to investigate. How does the data facet look? Run-on the title of the statistics casing would supply you the total table, on the other hand, you can likewise get the major n strains with DF. head(n) or the preserve going n strains with df.tail(n). df.shape would supply you the volume of traces and sections. df.info() would give you the list, data type and memory data. The order s.value_counts(dropna=False) would enable you to see fascinating traits and capability an association (like an area or a couple of segments). An especially useful course is df.describe() which facts, sources synopsis insights for numerical segments. It is additionally manageable to get measurements of the entire data define or an association (a section and so forth):

• df.mean()Returns the mean all matters considered

How about we currently figure mean shutting cost:

```
>>> df.loc['2012-Feb', 'Close'].mean()
```

528.4820021999999

In any case, should not something be said about express timespan?

```
>>> df.loc['2012-Feb':'2015-Feb', 'Close'].mean()
```

430.43968317018414

Would you like to recognize a suggest of shutting price via weeks? No prob.

```
>>> df.resample('W')['Close'].mean()
```

Date

2012-02-26 519.399979

2012-03-04 538.652008

2012-03-11 536.254004

2012-03-18 576.161993

2012-03-25 600.990001

2012-04-01 609.698003

2012-04-08 626.484993

2012-04-15 623.773999

2012-04-22 591.718002

2012-04-29 590.536005

2012-05-06 579.831995

2012-05-13 568.814001

2012-05-20 543.593996

2012-05-27 563.283995

2012-06-03 572.539994

2012-06-10 570.124002

2012-06-17 573.029991

2012-06-24 583.739993

2012-07-01 574.070004

2012-07-08 601.937489

2012-07-15 606.080008

2012-07-22 607.746011

2012-07-29 587.951999

2012-08-05 607.217999

2012-08-12 621.150003

2012-08-19 635.394003

2012-08-26 663.185999

2012-09-02 670.611995

2012-09-09 675.477503

2012-09-16 673.476007

...

2016-08-07 105.934003

2016-08-14 108.258000

2016-08-21 109.304001

2016-08-28 107.980000

2016-09-04 106.676001

2016-09-11 106.177498

2016-09-18 111.129999

2016-09-25 113.606001

2016-10-02 113.029999

2016-10-09 113.303999

2016-10-16 116.860000

2016-10-23 117.160001

2016-10-30 115.938000

2016-11-06 111.057999

2016-11-13 109.714000

2016-11-20 108.563999

2016-11-27 111.637503

2016-12-04 110.587999

2016-12-11 111.231999

2016-12-18 115.094002

2016-12-25 116.691998

2017-01-01 116.642502

2017-01-08 116.672501

2017-01-15 119.228000

2017-01-22 119.942499

2017-01-29 121.164000

2017-02-05 125.867999

2017-02-12 131.679996

2017-02-19 134.978000

2017-02-26 136.904999

Freq: W-SUN, Name: Close, dtype: float64

Resampling is an incredible asset with regards to time association examination. On the off danger that you need to locate out about resampling sense free to bounce into authority docs.

Representation in pandas

At the earliest reference point of this put up I said that pandas is based on Numpy, with regards to representation pandas utilizes library referred to as matplotlib. We should identify how Apple inventory prices change after some time on a diagram:

Taking Shutting cost between Feb, 2012 and Feb, 2017:

```
>>> import matplotlib.pyplot as plt

>>> new_sample_df = df.loc['2012-Feb':'2017-Feb', ['Close']]

>>> new_sample_df.plot()

>>> plt.show()
```

Estimations of X-pivot are spoken to via file estimations of DataFrame (as a count number of directions on the off danger that you don't give expressly), Y-hub is a cease cost. Investigate

2014, there is a drop in light of 7 to 1 breaks upheld by using Apple.

By what method Would panda be in a position to Be Utilized with Python

Pandas is a typical Python instrument for statistics manipulate and investigation. This venture discloses how to go via Pilot to set and begin working with Pandas in your selection of terminal, Python, IPython, or Jupyter Scratch pad. The potential is similar for introducing and opening nearly any bundle.

1. Start Pilot.

2. Click the Situations tab.

3. Click the Make catch. Whenever provoked, enter a picture identify for the earth, for example, "Pandas."

4. Select a Python adaptation to preserve jogging in the earth.

5. Click alright.

The new situation indicates up in the conditions listed.

6. Click the identify of the new circumstance to actuate it.

Nature is featured with an inexperienced foundation.

7. In the rundown over the bundles table, choose All to channel the desk to demonstrate all bundles in all channels.

8. In the Hunt Bundles box, type Pandas.

9. Pandas indicate up as a bundle handy for establishment.

10. Select the checkbox earlier than the Pandas bundle name.

11. In the menu that shows up, pick out Imprint for express variant establishment.

12. In the rundown that suggests up,

A development bar suggests up underneath the Bundles sheet while Pandas and its conditions are introduced.

To start utilizing your new condition, click the Situations tab.

Snap the bolt size with the aid of the Pandas condition name.

In the rundown list that indicates up, pick the device to use to open Pandas: Terminal, Python, IPython or Jupyter Journal.

Chapter 5: How to Use Python Data Analysis with Practical Examples

Python is a language that enables you to make snappy and primary code to do typically complicated assignments. It is regular to utilize the intuitive python translator to enter a couple of instructions so as to "make feel of" how they work. On the off hazard that you have finished any kind of indispensable python educational exercise, there will be a stage proper off the bat in the technique that requests that you type python in your path line.

The python route opens up a translator which allows you to kind instructions and get consistent enter on the outcomes. Here is a fundamental model from superb jokes:

$ python

Python 2.7.6 (default, Blemish 22 2014, 22:59:56)

[GCC 4.8.2] on linux2

Type "help", "copyright", "credits" or "permit" for greater data.

```
>>> import pprint

>>> pprint.pprint(zip(('Byte', 'KByte', 'MByte', 'GByte', 'TByte'),
(1 << 10*i for I in xrange(5))))

[('Byte', 1),
('KByte', 1024),
('MByte', 1048576),
('GByte', 1073741824),
('TByte', 1099511627776)]
>>>
```

While this intuitive circumstance is extraordinarily helpful, it is not favorable for step by step exhaustive investigation of python. In all respects from the get-go into your python venture, you may most possibly seize the wind of IPython. IPython offers several valuable highlights, including:

- tab ending
- object investigation
- command records

You can conjure ipython likewise alternatively you will right now, see a little special interface:

```
$ ipython
Python 2.7.6 (default, Blemish 22 2014, 22:59:56)
Type "copyright", "credits" or "permit" for more data.
IPython 2.3.0 - An Upgraded Intuitive Python.


? - > Presentation and plan of IPython's highlights.


%quickref - > Snappy reference.
help - > Python's very personal assistance framework.


object? - > Insights related to 'object', use 'object??' for extra
```

subtleties.

In [1]: import pprint

In [2]: pprint.pprint(zip(('Byte', 'KByte', 'MByte', 'GByte', 'TByte'), (1 << 10*i for I in xrange(5))))

```
[('Byte', 1),
('KByte', 1024),
('MByte', 1048576),
('GByte', 1073741824),
('TByte', 1099511627776)]
```
In [3]: help(pprint)
In [4]: pprint.

pprint.PrettyPrinter pprint.isrecursive pprint.pprint
pprint.warnings

pprint.isreadable pprint.pformat pprint.saferepr
In [4]: pprint.

In the model, I ran similar instructions to get a similar yield yet in addition attempted the assistance work simply as utilized TABcompletion in the wake of composing pprint. The other course I utilized was the up bolt to seem to be through the historic backdrop of directions, alter them and execute the outcomes:

In [4]: pprint.pprint(zip(('Byte', 'KiloByte', 'MegaByte', 'GigaByte', 'TeraByte'), (1 << 10*i for I in xrange(5))))

[('Byte', 1),
('KiloByte', 1024),
('MegaByte', 1048576),
('GigaByte', 1073741824),
('TeraByte', 1099511627776)]

In [5]: pprint.pprint(zip(('Byte', 'KByte', 'MByte', 'GByte', 'TByte'), (1 << 10*i for I in xrange(5))))

[('Byte', 1),

('KByte', 1024),

('MByte', 1048576),

('GByte', 1073741824),

('TByte', 1099511627776)]

IPython likewise makes it easy to become acquainted with the articles you are utilizing. On the off danger that you ever stall out, have a go at making use of the ? to grow to be acquainted with something:

In [9]: s = {'1','2'}

In [10]: s?

Type: set

String structure: set(['1', '2'])

Length: 2

Docstring:

set() - > new void set object

set(iterable) - > new set article

Fabricate an unordered gathering of specific components.

In [11]:

The usefulness given through IPython is surely cool and valuable and I urge you to introduce it on your framework and play with the exclusive highlights to get acquainted with it.

IPython Note pad

IPython is valuable and I have utilized it for the duration of the years when taking a shot at Django ventures. At some point in

2011, they presented the thinking of the IPython journal to this beneficial asset. For motives unknown I'm late to the gathering on the other hand due to the fact that I've gotten the probability to make use of them and play with them, I can see their great power.

The easiest strategy to depict an IPython Note pad is that it is an overly cool method to supply the IPython support in a program. Be that as it may, it does not definitely give IPython-like highlights in a program, it makes it extremely convenient to document your capacity and provide them with others. With regards to business applications, there are two central things to remember:

• Notebooks allow you to efficaciously interface with and look into your facts

• The investigation is virtually self-recording and permits you to successfully share and prepare others on what you are doing

Envision you are working with Exceed expectations, and have pretty recently made a turn desk or finished some distinctive examination. On the off threat that you would possibly favor to expose to any individual how to do it, what would you possibly do? Reorder screen pictures into Word? Record the session through some sort of screen recording instrument? Give them the Exceed expectations record and guide them to go make sense of it?

None of those selections are especially exquisite alternatively are truthfully the preferred in many spots the place Exceed expectations manages the in particular appointed investigation world. Python Scratch pad in a joint effort with pandas gives a vigorous technique to check out a lot of information and provide your system with your colleagues.

Python Information Examination Library

The Python Information Examination Library in any other case recognised as pandas is a "BSD-authorized library giving elite, simple to-utilize data constructions and information investigation apparatuses for the Python programming language." Pandas is an extraordinarily modern application and you can do some uncontrollably perplexing math with it. In future articles, I'll ride it in more element, then again, I wished to complete a quick example examination using comparable information I utilized in my sets article.

Beginning Up The earth

Begin a python journal session:

```
$ ipython notebook
```

Your program must then naturally open and divert to the journal server. Here is what the precept display resembles (yours will most possibly be vacant yet this demonstrates a couple of models observe pods):

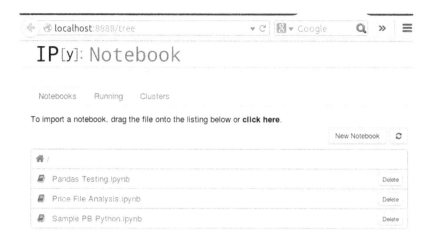

Tapping on the New Scratch pad catch starts another

circumstance for you to code:

You'll see that the records mobile looks specially like the

IPython direction short, we took a gander at before.

For the rest of this article, I will reveal the extraordinary

directions I have entered in the cells. I have downloaded, the

total session through means of rest so it coordinates all the extra flawlessly with my blog work process. On the off chance that people may desire the real scratch pad and additionally information records, let me understand and I'll submit them.

Also, the IPython Scratch pad has a ton of fantastic highlights. On the off danger that you would like me to discuss through it in greater element - encompass your contribution to the remarks. I was on hand for giving greater know-how into making use of this application.

Quick Information Examination with Pandas

Since I am thoroughly operational with my observe pad, I can do some quite groundbreaking investigation.

To begin with, we have to import the popular pandas libraries

import pandas as pd

import numpy as np

Next, we can peruse in the instance information and get a synopsis of what it appears like.

SALES=pd.read_csv("sample-sales.csv")

SALES.head()

Record Number Account Name sku category quantity   unit price ext price date

0 803666 Fritsch-Glover HX-24728 Belt   1   98.98 98.98 2014-09-28 11:56:02

1 64898 O'Conner Inc   LK-02338 Shirt   9   34.80 313.20 2014-04-24 16:51:22

2   423621   Beatty and Sons   ZC-07383   Shirt 12   60.24 722.88   2014-09-17 17:26:22

3   137865   Gleason, Bogisich and Franecki QS-76400   Shirt 5   15.25 76.25 2014-01-30 07:34:02

4   435433   Morissette-Heathcote   RU-25060   Shirt 19   51.83 984.77   2014-08-24 06:18:12

Presently, we can make use of the rotate desk potential to abridge the deals and radically change the strains of information into something helpful. We will begin with something simple

report =
SALES.pivot_table(values=['quantity'],index=['Account Name'],columns=['category'], aggfunc=np.sum)

report.head(n=10)

	Amount		
		Shirt	Shoes
Category	Belt		
Record Name		18	NaN
Abbott PLC	NaN	13	NaN
Abbott, Rogahn and Bednar	NaN	36	NaN
Abshire LLC	NaN	NaN	NaN
Altenwerth, Feeds and Paucek	NaN	NaN	11

This command shows us the number of products each customer purchased - all in one command! As impressive as this is, you'll notice that there are a bunch of NaN's in the output. This means "Not a Number" and represents places where there is no value.

Wouldn't it be nicer if the value was a 0 instead? That's where **fill_value** comes in:

report =
SALES.pivot_table(values=['quantity'],index=['Account Name'],columns=['category'], fill_value=0, aggfunc=np.sum)

report.head(n=10)

amount

Conclusion

Hello there! It's great to see that you successfully made it to the end of ***Python for Data Analysis!***

Whether you are an experienced programmer or are just starting out with Python, you will still need to know where to start. Python is one of, if not, the easiest programming languages to learn. So make sure to take notes as you explore what you need to start.

Install Python

The install of Python is an easy process and is normally included a recent Python edition with all Unix and Linux systems. A lot of computers from HP with Windows installed even have Python pre-installed. For those of you who have installed Python yourselves, but are confused with any of it you can go to the Python wiki page to review the download steps in the beginner's guide.

Learning Python

After you have Python successfully installed, you will now need to learn everything there is to learn about the popular programming language. First, you need to know which text editors and IDEs are best tailored to help with ease of editing.

The Python wiki page also provides many tutorials for programmers who are experienced. Not only that, but there are many other languages that Python supports if you do not speak English.

To get the most up to date information, you should take a look at their online docs. You'll find a tutorial filled with information that is both basic and brief that will help the starting process easy for you.

Finally, if you found this book useful in any way, a review on Amazon is always appreciated!